U.S. DEPARTMENT OF HOMELAND SECURITY

IMPLEMENTING

9/11

COMMISSION

RECOMMENDATIONS

Progress Report 2011

Table of Contents

Executive Summary

Overview

The United States has made significant progress in securing the nation from terrorism since the September 11, 2001 attacks. Nevertheless, work remains as the terrorist threats facing the country have evolved in the last ten years, and continue to change.

Following 9/11, the federal government moved quickly to develop a security framework to protect our country from large-scale attacks directed from abroad, while enhancing federal, state, and local capabilities to prepare for, respond to, and recover from threats and disasters at home. A key element of this framework included the creation of the Department of Homeland Security (DHS) in March, 2003, bringing together 22 separate agencies and offices into a single, Cabinet-level department[1].

Created with the founding principle of protecting the American people from terrorist and other threats, DHS and its many partners across the Federal government, public and private sectors, and communities throughout the country have strengthened the homeland security enterprise to better mitigate and defend against dynamic threats.

Many of the features of this new, more robust enterprise align with – and respond to – recommendations contained in the 9/11 Commission Report, released in July 2004 to assess the circumstances surrounding 9/11 and to identify ways to guard against future terrorist attacks.

In recognition of the 9/11 Commission Report and the tenth anniversary of 9/11, this report describes how DHS has addressed specific 9/11 Commission recommendations over the past ten years, making America stronger and more resilient. While challenges remain, the Department continues to focus on minimizing risks while maximizing the ability to respond and recover from attacks and disasters of all kinds. This is a challenge that the men and women of DHS commit themselves to everyday.

Progress Addressing Key Recommendations of the 9/11 Commission

Expanding Information Sharing

The United States' strengthened homeland security enterprise includes a number of critical features to expand and enhance information sharing that did not exist on 9/11. These include:

- 72 recognized fusion centers throughout the country, which serve as focal points for the receipt, analysis, gathering, and sharing of threat-related information between the federal government and state, local, tribal, territorial and private sector partners;

---

[1] Initiated by the passage of the Homeland Security Act of 2002 (Public Law 107-296).

U.S. Department of Homeland Security: Implementing 9/11 Commission Recommendations

- The Nationwide Suspicious Activity Reporting Initiative, which trains state and local law enforcement to recognize behaviors and indicators related to terrorism, crime and other threats and standardizes how those observations are documented, analyzed and shared with the federal government and other communities throughout the country;

- The National Terrorism Advisory System, which provides timely, detailed information about terrorist threats and recommended security measures to the public, government agencies, first responders, transportation hubs, and the private sector;

- The "If You See Something Say Something™" campaign—a program to raise public awareness of indicators of terrorism and crime, and emphasize the importance of reporting suspicious activity to the proper law enforcement authorities; and

- Robust information sharing with international partners, facilitating the exchange of information about terrorists and criminals.

Developing and Implementing Risk-based Transportation Security Strategies

DHS has made significant advances in risk-based security since 9/11, focusing on intelligence-driven, layered security across all transportation modes. This approach emphasizes pre-screening for passengers and cargo, while focusing resources on those who pose the greatest threat to the nation's transportation networks. Advances include:

- Conducting baseline security assessments across aviation, maritime, surface transportation sectors;

- Forging international consensus on historic new global aviation standards;

- Strengthening the security of the global supply chain;

- Collecting and analyzing advanced passenger and cargo information; and

- Supporting risk-based state and local prevention efforts.

Strengthening Airline Passenger Pre-screening and Targeting Terrorist Travel

Ten years ago, screening of passengers coming to the United States was limited to the visa process and inspection of a person by an immigration officer at the port of entry. Provision of Advance Passenger Information was voluntary. In response to both 9/11 and evolving threats, and with the help and support of Congress, DHS has significantly adapted and enhanced its ability to detect threats through a multi-layered, risk-based system. Today, DHS requires all airlines flying to the United States from foreign countries to provide Advance Passenger Information and Passenger Name Records prior to departure; checks 100 percent of passengers on flights flying to, from, or within the United States against government watchlists through its Secure Flight program; and has expanded trusted traveler programs, expediting travel for passengers who provide biometric identification and pass rigorous, recurrent security checks.

Enhancing Screening for Explosives

Prior to 9/11, limited federal security requirements existed for cargo or baggage screening. Today all checked and carry-on baggage is screened for explosives. The capacity of frontline security personnel and new technologies also has significantly expanded. In March 2002, TSA's first cadre of federal screeners totaled 80 individuals; today more than 52,000 TSA personnel serve on the frontlines at over 450 U.S. airports. Through the Recovery Act and annual appropriations, TSA has accelerated the deployment of new technologies to detect the next generation of threats. Additionally, TSA continues to work closely with state and local law enforcement to support surface transportation security through the deployment of Visible Intermodal Prevention and Response Teams, which provide deterrent and detection capabilities across all modes of transportation to prevent or disrupt potential attacks.

Protecting Cyber Networks and Critical Physical Infrastructure

DHS has made significant strides to enhance the security of the nation's critical physical infrastructure as well as its cyber infrastructure and networks. Current tools include the National Cybersecurity Protection System, of which the EINSTEIN cyber intrusion detection system is a key component; the National Cybersecurity and Communications Integration Center, which serves as the nation's principal hub for organizing cyber response efforts; a 2010 landmark agreement between DHS and the Department of Defense to align and enhance America's capabilities to protect against threats to critical civilian and military computer systems and networks; the National Infrastructure Protection Plan, a comprehensive risk management framework for all levels of government, private industry, nongovernmental entities and tribal partners; and implementation of the Chemical Facility Anti-Terrorism Standards to regulate security at high-risk chemical facilities. Additionally, in February 2011, President Obama announced the Wireless Innovation and Infrastructure Initiative to develop and deploy a nationwide, interoperable wireless network for public safety. None of these tools existed prior to 9/11.

Bolstering the Security of U.S. Borders and Identification Documents

Protecting the nation's borders—land, air, and sea—from the illegal entry of people, weapons, drugs, and contraband is vital to homeland security, as well as the nation's economic prosperity. Over the past several years, DHS has deployed unprecedented levels of personnel, technology, and resources to the Southwest border, and made critical security improvements along the Northern and maritime borders. Additionally, DHS has taken significant steps to strengthen the security, reliability and accuracy of personal identification documents and reduce identity fraud while enhancing privacy safeguards, including fundamentally transforming the way travelers enter the country through the Western Hemisphere Travel Initiative and preventing potential terrorist and criminal threats from coming to the United States through the Visa Security Program, Visa Waiver Program and other pre-departure measures.

Ensuring Robust Privacy and Civil Rights and Civil Liberties Safeguards

DHS has the first statutorily required privacy office of any federal agency, and the Department builds privacy and civil rights and civil liberties protections into its operations, policies, programs, and technology deployments from the outset of their development. The DHS Privacy Office partners with every DHS component to assess policies, programs, systems, technologies, and rule-makings for privacy risks, and recommends privacy protections and methods for handling personally identifiable information. DHS's Office for Civil Rights and Civil Liberties plays a key role in the Department's mission to secure the nation while preserving individual freedoms through the Civil Rights and Civil Liberties Impact Assessment process. It also engages with communities across the country on civil rights and civil liberties issues.

Challenges that Remain

While DHS has made great progress in securing the nation since the September 11, 2001 attacks, challenges remain in implementing key recommendations in the 9/11 Commission Report. Despite significant efforts, including the proposed PASS ID legislation to enhance the security of driver's licenses, many states are still unable to fulfill the congressionally mandated REAL ID requirements. The Department also continues to undertake new steps to increase the use of risk-based security screening; develop strategies to guard against an increasing volume of cyber attacks; partner with first responders to address interoperability challenges; determine a cost-effective means to implement a biometric exit solution; and guard against potential spillover effects of drug cartel violence in Northern Mexico.

While the demands on DHS have never been greater, the current fiscal climate requires the Department to continue to maximize every security dollar. In order to preserve front line security operations, DHS has identified over $1 billion in cost avoidances and cuts under this Administration. In addition, the Department's fiscal year 2012 budget request included more than $800 million in further reductions associated with administrative savings and efficiency initiatives currently underway, from efforts to reform acquisition, asset and real property management to cuts to professional services contracts, supplies and materials, printing, and travel.

Conclusion

While America is stronger and more resilient as a result of these efforts to strengthen the homeland security enterprise, threats from terrorism persist and continue to evolve. Today's threats do not come from any one individual or group. They may originate in distant lands or local neighborhoods. They may be as simple as a homemade bomb or as sophisticated as a biological threat or coordinated cyber attack.

More and more, state, local, and tribal law enforcement officers, as well as citizens, businesses, and communities are on the frontlines of detection and prevention. Protecting the nation is a shared responsibility and everyone can contribute by staying informed and aware of the threats the country faces. Homeland security starts with hometown security—and we all have a role to play.

U.S. Department of Homeland Security: Implementing 9/11 Commission Recommendations

September 11 Chronology

September 11, 2001	Today
In early 1999, Osama Bin Laden summoned operatives to Afghanistan to discuss using commercial aircraft as weapons and developed a list of potential targets in the United States.	Today, in concert with public and private sector partners as well as international allies, this Administration has developed a multi-layered information sharing security strategy to target and identify both known and unknown individuals that may pose a threat to the United States wherever the operational planning might occur with the goal of preventing such persons from entering the country.
In April of 1999, the hijackers began to obtain passports and visas for travel to the United States.	DHS and other federal partners have built a capacity to more extensively vet those individuals applying for visas or travel to the U.S. For example, through the Visa Security Program, which did not exist on 9/11 and is now operational at 19 posts in 15 countries, Immigration and Customs Enforcement, in conjunction with the State Department, deploys trained special agents overseas to high-risk visa activity posts to conduct targeted, in-depth reviews of particular visa applications and applicants before they reach the United States.
Between 1999 and 2001, many of the hijackers prepared for the 9/11 attack while living in Germany.	The Department of Homeland Security (DHS), in collaboration with the Departments of Justice and State, has signed Preventing and Combating Serious Crime Agreements with 18 countries, including Germany, to share information about terrorists and criminals.
The hijackers began arriving in the U.S. in late April 2001 on tourist visas with cash and travelers checks acquired in the Middle East.	DHS partners with the Terrorist Screening Center, the National Counterterrorism Center and other federal entities to analyze travel-related data in order to better understand and anticipate the travel patterns of known or suspected terrorists. Today's travel related databases along with threat-related intelligence have been essential in identifying, targeting, and interdicting known and suspected terrorists as well as suspicious cargo before it enters the United States.
Prior to 9/11, the hijackers enrolled in flight schools and conducted cross-country surveillance flights in order to identify aircraft that would produce their desired impact.	The Transportation Security Administration (TSA) has responsibility for ensuring that foreign students seeking training at flight schools do not pose a threat to aviation or national security. TSA performs background checks, including government watchlist matching, a criminal history check, and an immigration status check.
During the spring and summer of 2001, several of the hijackers were apprehended by U.S. law	Today, 72 recognized fusion centers throughout the country serve as focal points at the state and local level for the receipt, analysis,

U.S. Department of Homeland Security: Implementing 9/11 Commission Recommendations

enforcement for various traffic violations.	gathering, and sharing of threat and vulnerability-related information. In addition, the Nationwide Suspicious Activity Reporting Initiative helps to train state and local law enforcement to recognize behaviors and indicators related to terrorism, crime and other threats while standardizing how those observations are analyzed and disseminated. Finally, state and local law enforcement officers can determine whether an individual is on a watchlist through the National Crime Information Center.
On the morning of 9/11, hijackers passed through security checkpoints at four U.S. airports, allegedly carrying knives, box cutters and concealed weapons on their person or in carry-on luggage.	Multilayered security measures are now in place to enhance aviation security including the prescreening of passengers; the deployment of new technologies; and training of airport security and law enforcement personnel to better detect behaviors associated with terrorism. Since 9/11, the capacity of frontline security personnel and new technologies has significantly expanded. Through Secure Flight, DHS now prescreens 100% of the 14 million passengers flying weekly to, from, and within the U.S. against government watchlists. In addition, all checked and carry-on baggage is now screened for metallic and non-metallic threats by new technologies as well as over 52,000 transportation security officers at more than 450 airports across the country.
Although eight of the hijackers were randomly selected for additional screening and a gate agent flagged two as suspicious, none were prevented from boarding their flights on 9/11.	Today, TSA's Behavior Detection Officers utilize non-intrusive behavior observation and analysis techniques to identify potentially high-risk passengers who exhibit behaviors that indicate they may be a threat to aviation and/or transportation security and refer them for additional screening. TSA also conducts screening of passengers at boarding gates based on current intelligence and passengers of interest.
At 8:19 AM, flight attendants and passengers began reporting hijackings of the aircraft via airphone.	Following 9/11, all commercial aircraft have been secured through the hardening of cockpit doors. In addition, the risk-based deployment of Federal Air Marshals, the Federal Flight Deck Officer program, in which eligible flight crewmembers are authorized by TSA to use firearms to defend against violence, and the crewmember behavior recognition and response training program, all provide additional layers of aviation security.
Throughout the morning of September 11, 2011, air traffic control operators, military personnel and first responders on the ground lacked situational awareness of what other agencies were doing to address the developing crisis.	Through the use of mobile and fixed site technologies, voice radio systems used by first responders are more interoperable than ever before. Since 9/11, the federal government has made significant organizational changes and investments in training and technical assistance to improve emergency communications capabilities. Moreover, the National Emergency Communications Plan and Incident Command System have established standardized plans, protocols, and procedures to improve command, control, and communications.

U.S. Department of Homeland Security: Implementing 9/11 Commission Recommendations

Introduction: Strengthening the Homeland Security Enterprise to Address Evolving Threats

The United States has made important progress in securing the nation from terrorism since the September 11, 2001 attacks.

After 9/11, the federal government moved quickly to develop a security framework to protect the country from the kind of large-scale attack, directed from abroad, that struck the nation nearly ten years ago. This framework has led to considerable success in both preventing this kind of attack and limiting, though not eliminating, the operational ability of the core al-Qa'ida group.

Nevertheless, work remains as threats from terrorism persist and continue to evolve. While Osama bin Laden is now dead, the United States continues to face threats from al-Qa'ida and other terrorist groups inspired by al-Qa'ida or other extremist ideology. In addition, the nation must address threats that are homegrown as well as those that emanate from abroad.

Over the past several years, the Department of Homeland Security (DHS) and our partners have worked to strengthen and evolve the homeland security enterprise to better defend against evolving terrorist threats. This new approach contains several dimensions.

Within the federal government, many departments and agencies contribute to the homeland security mission. The nation's armed forces, while often stationed thousands of miles away, are on the frontlines of homeland security by helping to significantly degrade al-Qa'ida capabilities to attack the United States and targets throughout the world. The Director of National Intelligence, the Central Intelligence Agency, and the entire Intelligence Community, of which DHS is a member, is producing more and better streams of intelligence than before. Multiple federal departments and agencies, including the Terrorist Screening Center (TSC) and the National Counterterrorism Center (NCTC) have made critical enhancements to the federal watchlisting systems and to the coordination of the federal government's counterterrorism efforts. The federal homeland security enterprise also includes the strong presence of the Department of Justice (DOJ) and the Federal Bureau of Investigation (FBI), whose role in leading terrorism investigations has led to the arrest of more than two-dozen Americans on terrorism-related charges since 2009.

The homeland security enterprise extends far beyond DHS and the federal government. A key part of the enterprise includes working directly with law enforcement, state and local leaders, community-based organizations, and private sector partners to counter violent extremism at its source, using many of the same techniques and strategies that have proven successful for decades in combating violent crime in American communities.

Further, DHS has focused on getting resources and information out of Washington, D.C. and into the hands of state and local law enforcement[2], to provide them with the tools they need to identify

---

[2] "Local" law enforcement in this Report includes all law enforcement at the municipal, tribal and territorial levels.

and address threats in their communities. Because state and local law enforcement are often in the best position to notice the first signs of a planned attack, homeland security efforts must be integrated into the police work that they do every day, providing officers on the front lines with a clear understanding of the tactics, behaviors, and other indicators that could point to terrorist activity.

DHS supports these efforts through robust information sharing with public and private sector partners; fusion centers to build analytical capability at the state and local level; participation in the Nationwide Suspicious Activity Reporting Initiative (NSI) and FBI-led Joint Terrorism Task Forces (JTTF); and grants, training, and technical assistance that DHS provides to its state and local partners.

The public also plays a key role in this new homeland security enterprise. Through the nationwide expansion of the "If You See Something, Say Something™" campaign, DHS is raising public awareness of indicators of terrorism, crime and other threats while emphasizing the importance of reporting suspicious activity to the proper law enforcement authorities. Recently, DHS replaced the color-coded alert system, created shortly after the 9/11 attacks, with the new National Terrorism Advisory System (NTAS)—a robust terrorism advisory system that provides timely information to the public and the private sector, as well as to state, local, and tribal governments about credible terrorist threats and recommended security measures.

DHS also works closely with international partners, including major multilateral organizations and global businesses to strengthen the security of the networks of global trade and travel upon which the nation's economy and communities rely. DHS has enhanced the security of the aviation system, not only in airports throughout the United States, but also in airports abroad, by working directly with foreign governments, international organizations, and the aviation industry to raise aviation security standards. The Administration's global supply chain initiative is building on many of these partnerships, including work with International Civil Aviation Organization (ICAO), World Customs Organization (WCO) and International Maritime Organization (IMO).

Taken together, these multi-layered efforts provide a strong foundation that DHS, the public, federal, state, local, private sector, and international partners can all use to protect communities from terrorism and other threats. The homeland security enterprise is further strengthened by continuing efforts to better understand the risks confronting the homeland, and to engage the international community, while protecting the fundamental rights of all Americans.

Expanding Information Sharing

RECOMMENDATION: Provide Incentives for Information Sharing[3]

Over the past several years, DHS has strengthened and evolved our homeland security enterprise to better mitigate and defend against dynamic threats. This approach is based on the simple premise that homeland security begins with hometown security. Through close partnerships with federal, state and local governments, community-based organizations, and private sector partners, DHS works to ensure that resources and information are available to state and local law enforcement, giving those on the frontlines the tools they need to protect local communities. This approach includes a number of critical features that did not exist prior to 9/11. Simply put, DHS is focused on assembling information and sharing it across the country in a way best designed to protect the homeland.

National Terrorism Advisory System

In April 2011, DHS announced the implementation of the new NTAS, replacing the former color-coded alert system, which had become obsolete. NTAS is designed to more effectively communicate information about terrorist threats by providing timely, detailed information and recommended security measures to the public, government agencies, first responders, airports and other transportation hubs, and the private sector.

Under NTAS, DHS will coordinate with other federal entities to issue detailed alerts to the public when the federal government receives information about a specific, credible terrorist threat to the United States. NTAS alerts provide a concise summary of the potential threat, which may include a geographic region, mode of transportation, or critical infrastructure potentially affected by the threat; actions being taken to ensure public safety; and recommended steps that individuals, communities, business and governments can take to help prevent, mitigate or respond to a threat. NTAS Alerts contain a sunset provision indicating a specific date when the alert expires.

Information Sharing

In the ten years since 9/11, the federal government has strengthened the connection between collection and analysis on transnational organizations and threats. Terrorism-related information sharing across the intelligence community has greatly improved, and through the establishment of the DHS Office of Intelligence & Analysis (I&A), we have strengthened the ability to convey intelligence on threats to the homeland in a context that is useful and relevant to law enforcement and homeland security officials at the state and local level.

---

[3] 9/11 Commission Report, pg. 417

DHS, working closely with the FBI, has re-focused its information sharing and production efforts to better address the needs of state and local governments and private sector partners. DHS consults with law enforcement officials from major metropolitan areas, the directors of fusion centers, and State Homeland Security Advisors to tailor the Department's products and briefings to better support state and local law enforcement.

Consistent with the direction the President has set for a robust information sharing environment, DHS provides, in coordination with the FBI, regular training programs for local law enforcement to help them identify indicators of terrorist activity. In addition, DHS continues to improve and expand the information-sharing mechanisms by which officers are made aware of the threat picture, vulnerabilities, and what it means for their local communities.

Countering Violent Extremism

One example of the Department's efforts to work with state and local officials, as well as community groups, is focused on Countering Violent Extremism (CVE). Over the past year, DHS has worked with its partners to develop a training curriculum for state and local law enforcement that is focused on community-oriented policing to help frontline personnel identify activities that are indicators of potential terrorist activity and violence. In conjunction with local communities and DOJ, DHS has published guidance on best practices for community partnerships to prevent and mitigate homegrown threats. DHS has also participated in dozens of community roundtable discussions and trained more than 2,300 state and local personnel on CVE related topics.

Fusion Centers

DHS also supports state and major urban area fusion centers, which interact regularly with JTTFs and serve as focal points within the state and local environment for the receipt, analysis, gathering, and sharing of threat-related information including classified intelligence. Fusion centers are uniquely situated to empower front-line law enforcement, public safety, fire service, emergency response, public health, critical infrastructure protection, and private sector security personnel to understand local implications of national intelligence, thus enabling local officials to better protect their communities.

While fusion centers did not exist ten years ago, today there are 72 recognized fusion centers throughout the country that receive support from the federal government through personnel, training, technical assistance, security clearances, connectivity to federal systems, technology, and grant funding. DHS has deployed Homeland Secure Data Network systems to fusion centers, enabling the federal government to share information and intelligence—including classified terrorism-related threat information—with state, local, tribal, territorial, and private sector partners. DHS has also placed federal intelligence officers at fusion centers, who act as the primary liaison between the federal governments and its partners.

Federal Partners

DHS works closely with its partners across the federal government on various information sharing initiatives to support law enforcement operations and protect the country from terrorists and other threats.

A critical partner for DHS, JTTFs are led by the FBI and coordinate resources and expertise from across the federal government to investigate terrorism cases. DHS has provided hundreds of personnel, including U.S. Immigration and Custom Enforcement (ICE) special agents, U.S. Secret Service (USSS) agents, Federal Air Marshals, U.S. Customs and Border Protection (CBP) officers, U.S. Citizenship and Immigration Services (USCIS) officers and representatives from the Federal Emergency Management Agency (FEMA) and the U.S. Coast Guard (USCG), to support the 104 JTTFs across the country. JTTFs have been critical to many recent terrorism investigations, including the arrests of Najibullah Zazi and Faisal Shahzad for terrorist plots to attack the New York transit system and Times Square, respectively.

Tribal Partners

The Obama Administration has focused on building strong relationships with Tribal governments and law enforcement across the nation. In 2009, DHS designated Tribal liaisons in every operational component to work directly with tribal communities, and in 2011, DHS announced a new DHS Tribal Consultation Policy outlining the guiding principles under which all elements of the Department are to engage with sovereign tribal governments.

Private Sector Partners

The private sector is an integral component of the homeland security enterprise, and through the Department's private sector office, DHS has worked to improve coordination of private sector engagement across the Department, facilitating more effective and rapid communication with key organizations and bolstering regionally-focused information sharing efforts.

International Engagement

The Administration has also expanded information sharing with its international partners. DHS, in collaboration with DOJ and the Department of State (DOS), has signed Preventing and Combating Serious Crime (PCSC) Agreements with 17 Visa Waiver Program (VWP) countries and one non-VWP country to share information about terrorists and criminals. Working closely with Australia, Canada, New Zealand, and the United Kingdom, DHS participates in biographic and biometric data exchange, which enables each country to query each other's fingerprint databases and voluntarily provide data about criminals and terrorists. These efforts, and the collection of Electronic System for Travel Authorization (ESTA) data required prior to VWP travel, allow DHS to identify and stop those who seek to defraud or exploit the legitimate systems of trade and travel. In addition, DHS has signed 12 international agreements to foster collaboration in science and technology, including research and development in cutting-edge technologies to ensure our mutual security. At the multilateral level, DHS has worked via ICAO to raise global aviation security standards and has partnered with ICAO, IMO, and the WCO to strengthen the standards for cargo security worldwide.

Nationwide Suspicious Activity Reporting Initiative

DHS has worked with its federal, state, local and private sector partners, to expand the Nationwide Suspicious Activity Reporting Initiative (NSI) —an administration effort to train state and local law enforcement to recognize behaviors and indicators related to terrorism, crime and other threats; standardize how those observations are documented and analyzed; and enhance the sharing of those reports with law enforcement and communities throughout the country. While NSI type capabilities did not exist on 9/11, the program is currently active in 25 states,[4] 13 major cities,[5] and with Amtrak.

To date, more than 46,000 frontline law enforcement personnel have received Suspicious Activity Reporting (SAR) training, with all frontline law enforcement personnel in the United States expected to receive this training by fall 2011, thanks to partnerships with the International Association of Chiefs of Police, the Major Cities Chiefs Association, the Major County Sheriffs' Association, and the National Sheriffs' Association. As part of Nationwide Suspicious Activity Reporting Initiative, specially trained DHS analysts review suspicious activity reporting and provide SAR-related intelligence products to fusion centers, JTTFs, and DHS operational components. In conjunction with the NSI, DHS is also working to provide reporting capability directly to owners and operators of critical infrastructure.

"If You See Something, Say Something™" Campaign

The public also plays a role in homeland security through the expansion of the "If You See Something, Say Something™" campaign—a simple and effective initiative, originally implemented by New York City's Metropolitan Transportation Authority, to raise public awareness of indicators of terrorism and crime, and emphasize the importance of reporting suspicious activity to law enforcement authorities. This campaign is being expanded to places where NSI is being implemented, to ensure that calls to authorities will be handled appropriately, in an environment where privacy and civil liberties protections are in place.

The "If You See Something, Say Something™" campaign has been launched in partnership with the National Collegiate Athletic Association, National Basketball Association, National Football League, Pentagon Force Protection Agency, Wal-Mart, Mall of America, American Hotel & Lodging

---

[4] Alabama, Arizona, Colorado, Delaware, Florida, Georgia, Indiana, Louisiana, Maryland, Massachusetts, Minnesota, Mississippi, Missouri, Nebraska, New Jersey, New York, Ohio, Pennsylvania, South Carolina, Tennessee, Texas, Utah, Virginia, Washington, and Wisconsin

[5] Boston, Chicago, Dallas, District of Columbia, Houston, Kansas City, MO, Las Vegas, Los Angeles, Miami, Milwaukee, Orlando, Phoenix, and San Francisco

Association, Amtrak, and the general aviation industry, as well as in more than 9,000 federal buildings, venues and stadiums, and state and local fusion centers across the country.

In collaboration with the "If You See Something, Say Something™" campaign, the Transportation Security Administration (TSA) also provides suspicious behavior observation, assessment, and reporting training through its First Observer™ initiative, launched in 2008, which has trained thousands of state and local law enforcement personnel and private sector employees to observe, detect and report suspicious behavior at transportation and critical infrastructure sites and facilities across the country.

Additionally, the USCG operates the America's Waterway Watch (AWW) Program, launched in 2005, to educate citizens about threats around America's waterfront areas, and provide a means for reporting suspicious activity to responsible authorities. Under AWW, USCG personnel work with maritime businesses, ports and government agencies and build educational awareness among the recreational boating public and marina operators.

Developing and Implementing Risk-Based Transportation Security Strategies

RECOMMENDATION: Develop a Risk-Based Plan for Transportation Security[6]

DHS focuses on risk-based, intelligence-driven security across all modes of transportation. This approach emphasizes pre-screening for passengers and cargo to expedite travel for individuals that law enforcement knows the most about, while focusing limited resources on those who pose the greatest threat to the nation's transportation networks. Significant advances in risk-based security include baseline security assessments across aviation, maritime, and surface transportation sectors; historic global aviation standards; advanced passenger and cargo information; and enhanced information sharing with international and private sector partners. In June 2010, TSA provided to Congress the Transportation Sector Security Risk Assessment report, a nationwide risk assessment that examines the potential threats, vulnerabilities, and consequences of a terrorist attack involving the nation's transportation system, including the aviation and surface domains. This report has informed the development of risk mitigation strategies, security standards, countermeasures, and resource allocations.

Aviation Security

International Engagement

After the attempted terrorist attack against Northwest Airlines Flight #253 on December 25, 2009, DHS worked with ICAO on an unprecedented initiative to strengthen global aviation against threats posed by terrorists, working in multilateral and bilateral contexts with governments as well as industry. Secretary Napolitano participated in regional aviation security summits around the world, bringing about consensus within the international community to strengthen the civil aviation system through enhanced information analysis and sharing, cooperation on technological development, and modernized aviation security standards.

These efforts culminated at the ICAO Triennial Assembly in October 2010, where nearly 190 countries of the Assembly adopted the Declaration on Aviation Security, which forges a historic new foundation for aviation security to better protect the entire global aviation system and make air travel safer and more secure than ever before. The Declaration is implemented through two agreements:

- The ICAO Comprehensive Aviation Security Strategy sets the course for ICAO's aviation security efforts over the next six years. This strategy promotes innovative, effective, and

---

[6] 9/11 Commission Report, pg. 391

efficient aviation security approaches that focus on information sharing, compliance, and oversight, and stresses the importance of security among all of ICAO's members and stakeholders; and

- The amendment to the ICAO security standards and recommended practices calls for the deployment of advanced security technology, the incorporation of random and unpredictable aviation security measures, and the implementation of enhanced screening and security measures for cargo, mail and the entire global supply chain.

While TSA does not conduct passenger screening abroad, it requires airports that serve as the last point of departure to the U.S. to meet stringent security standards. TSA also conducts international aviation security training for countries around the world, focusing on risk-based security strategies, including cargo security, screening techniques, vulnerability assessments and airport security management, among other topics. Finally, TSA has formalized 60 agreements with foreign governments permitting Federal Air Marshals on international U.S. carrier flights and more are currently underway.

Private Sector Engagement

Immediately following the thwarted terrorist plot to conceal and ship explosive devices on aircraft bound for the United States in October 2010, DHS worked with industry to implement additional precautionary security measures for international inbound flights. Today, DHS continues to work with leaders from global shipping companies and the International Air Transport Association (IATA) on developing preventative measures, including terrorism awareness training for employees and vetting personnel with access to cargo.

In December 2010, CBP, TSA, and the air cargo industry launched the Air Cargo Advance Screening Pilot to share electronic shipping information for international flights to the United States prior to departure to improve the identification of high-risk shipments. DHS also established a high level working group comprised of leaders in the express cargo and passenger airline industries, the U.S. Postal Service (USPS), IATA and the American Transport Association to develop new industry and government-wide best practices to secure cargo while ensuring the timely flow of cargo and mail.

To strengthen passenger safety, DHS has also worked with the airlines and flight attendant associations to develop a behavior recognition and response training program to teach flight crews how to detect, respond to, and report common indicators of suspicious activity. Initially developed in 2010, this course has been incorporated into the voluntary Crew Member Self Defense Training Program.

Additionally, in 2011, TSA began taking additional steps to streamline security screening for U.S. air carrier pilots through a program that verifies pilots' identity for expedited screening at airport checkpoints nationwide. TSA continues to explore ways to accelerate and field risk-based, intelligence-driven approaches to aviation and transportation security. This approach will place additional emphasis on pre-screening passengers to strengthen security and improve the passenger experience, building on its multi-layered approach to transportation security.

Surface Transportation Security

The transit sector, due to its open access architecture, has a fundamentally different operational environment than aviation. Accordingly, DHS helps secure surface transportation infrastructure through risk-based security assessments, critical infrastructure hardening, and close partnerships with state and local law enforcement partners.

Risk-Based Assessments

Recognizing that the risk from terrorism and other hazards to surface transportation requires a coordinated approach involving all sector partners and stakeholders, the Obama Administration initiated a comprehensive review of U.S. surface transportation security efforts across all modes in 2009. The resulting Surface Transportation Security Priority Assessment (STSPA), released in April 2010, identified interagency priorities for the next four years and provided concrete recommendations on how to enhance security efforts and maximize the use of partnerships to optimize public safety, facilitate commerce, and strengthen the resiliency of the country's surface transportation system.

DHS has completed risk-based implementation plans for each of the 20 consensus recommendations of the STSPA, addressing the potential risks to the surface transportation system and its four subsectors (mass transit and passenger rail, highways and motor carriers, freight rail, and pipelines). These plans focus on improving information sharing, increasing coordination among federal agencies involved in the transportation sector, and improving the effectiveness and efficiency of the grants process. As of July 2011, 10 recommendations have been fully implemented and implementation of the others is underway.

Since 2006, TSA has completed more than 190 Baseline Assessments for Security Enhancement for mass transit, which provides a comprehensive assessment of security programs in critical transit systems around the country. The results of these assessments inform the development of risk mitigation priorities, security enhancement programs, and resource allocations—notably transit security grants. As a result, significant progress has been achieved in the areas of critical infrastructure hardening; technology development and implementation; training, drills and exercises; emergency management and planning; and background investigations.

Additionally, DHS's Science and Technology Directorate (S&T) has conducted detailed vulnerability analyses for all U.S. underwater mass transit tunnels, the results of which have enabled transit agencies to better evaluate potential risk to their tunnels. These evaluations were also incorporated into TSA risk assessments for tunnels and are currently guiding efforts to develop protective countermeasures for mass transit infrastructure.

In an effort to further harden critical surface transportation infrastructure, in 2010, TSA, in coordination with the U.S. Department of Transportation (DOT), the U.S. Army Corp of Engineers, and other DHS offices, developed and implemented the "National Strategy for Highway Bridge Security," to conduct comprehensive structural security assessments on the nation's most significant highway structures, including bridges, tunnels and terminals. To date, TSA has completed 30 of these structural security assessments.

Supporting State and Local Efforts

Additionally, TSA has various programs designed to support state and local efforts to bolster surface transportation security. Through its 25 multi-modal Visible Intermodal Prevention and Response (VIPR) Teams, which are comprised of Federal Air Marshals, surface/aviation transportation security inspectors, Behavioral Detection Officers, Transportation Security Officers (TSO), and canine teams, TSA helps provide state and local law enforcement with deterrent and detection capabilities to prevent or disrupt potential terrorist planning activities. Since the VIPR program was created in 2008, there have been over 17,700 operations performed.

In addition, since 2006, DHS has awarded over $1.6 billion in Surface Transportation Security Grants to help protect the public and nation's critical transportation infrastructure against acts of terrorism and other large-scale events. These grants support high-impact security projects, such as operational deterrence and critical transit infrastructure hardening that have a high efficacy in reducing the risk to the nation's transportation systems. In 2011, DHS announced a new model for the Transit Security Grant Program, which focuses limited resources on hardening the highest risk "shovel ready" transit infrastructure, while prioritizing operational deterrence activities such as training, exercises, canine and mobile screening teams.

Maritime Transportation Security

DHS is focused on strengthening maritime transportation security through a risk- and technology-based approach by evaluating vulnerabilities and mitigating threats across all potential pathways.

To this end, the USCG has published a series of regulations to increase the security of U.S. ports, ships, and facilities. These regulations extend maritime domain awareness through long-range tracking, promote information sharing through Notice of Arrivals/Automatic Identification Systems, and standardize crew identification documents.

To support state and local efforts to strengthen maritime security, since fiscal year 2003, DHS has provided more than $2 billion in grants for the Port Security Grant Program (PSGP)—awarded based on risk—to protect critical port infrastructure from terrorism, enhance maritime domain awareness and risk management capabilities, and support the implementation of the Transportation Worker Identification Credential (TWIC).

Risk-Based Assessments of Maritime Transportation Security

Since 2006, the USCG has used the Maritime Security Risk Analysis Model (MSRAM) to conduct anti-terrorism risk assessments at the nation's ports in order to assess threat, vulnerability, and consequence factors for various potential terrorist attack scenarios.

The USCG has also established the International Port Security (IPS) Program to assess anti-terrorism measures in foreign ports that conduct maritime trade with the United States. In cases where the USCG finds that effective anti-terrorism measures are not in place, vessels arriving to the United States from those ports are required to implement additional security measures. To date, the IPS Program has assessed over 900 port facilities in more than 150 countries.

In addition, the USCG conducts intelligence-informed, risk-based Security Boardings to verify the identity of crew members and to ascertain if a vessel poses a threat to the port and whether it should be permitted or denied entry.

Maritime Transportation Security Operations and Training

USCG's Maritime Security and Response Operations include waterborne and aerial patrols as well as armed escorts of hazardous cargos and passenger vessels in order to reduce the risk of terrorism to the U.S. Marine Transportation System and critical infrastructure and key resources (CIKR). The USCG also utilizes advanced interdiction capabilities to interdict identified threats—including chemical, biological, radiological, nuclear, and explosives threats—before they reach the United States.

USCG has increased the presence and capabilities of maritime forces to address high risk threats through the establishment of the Deployable Operations Group, which can respond rapidly to terrorist and weapons of mass destruction threats as well as Maritime Safety and Security Teams at critical U.S. ports, which focus on domestic maritime threats and post-incident response.

The USCG utilizes United States Visitor and Immigrant Status Indicator Technology (US-VISIT) to provide mobile biometrics collection and analysis capability at sea, along with other remote areas where DHS operates. The USCG is actively working to expand its at-sea biometric capability to assist in the prosecution of persons engaged in illegal maritime activity including illegal migration, smuggling, and drug transportation.

The Federal Law Enforcement Training Center, which provides training to 90 federal agencies and more than 67,000 federal, state, and local law enforcement personnel each year, has also developed and enhanced maritime security training programs focused on physical security and antiterrorism techniques for port security, including the development of a first-of-its-kind maritime law enforcement training center in Los Angeles to train state and local law enforcement personnel in various maritime counterterrorism operations.

Maritime Cargo Security

Agencies throughout the Obama Administration are working collaboratively to develop a unified vision for global supply chain security across air, land, and sea modes of transportation. The implementation of this strategy, which the Administration anticipates completing in 2011, will more comprehensively address risk than ever before. As this effort progresses, DHS continues its ongoing research and development work to address some of the limitations inherent in available technology and to explore innovative next-generation capabilities. For example, DHS is working to develop mobile scanning systems and technologies with enhanced penetration capabilities to strengthen the ability to detect illicit materials in very dense cargo. DHS is also working to develop technologies that can automatically detect and analyze suspicious anomalies within cargo containers, mitigating the need for more time-consuming and challenging approaches.

CBP has also implemented the Container Security Initiative (CSI) to ensure that U.S.-bound maritime containers that pose a potential risk are identified and inspected before they are placed on vessels destined for the U.S. CSI, which was first announced in January 2002, is currently operational in 58 foreign seaports in 32 countries.

Finally, in January 2010, CBP began enforcement of the Importer Security Filing and Additional Carrier Requirements interim final rule—also known as the "10 + 2 rule"—increasing the scope and accuracy of information gathered on cargo shipments arriving by sea into the United States and bolstering DHS's layered enforcement strategy to protect against terrorism and other crimes at U.S. ports of entry.

Strengthening Airline Passenger Pre-Screening and Targeting Terrorist Travel

RECOMMENDATIONS: Improve airline passenger pre-screening[7] and target terrorist travel[8]

Prior to 9/11, screening of passengers coming to the United States was limited to the DOS visa process and the inspection of a person by an immigration officer at the port of entry. Provision of advance passenger information (API) by airlines was voluntary and often inconsistent. Over the past ten years, DHS has significantly adapted and enhanced its ability to detect threats, building a layered, risk-based system that includes a full range of identification verification measures – from visa application checks and biometric identification to the receipt of advanced passenger information and the full implementation of Secure Flight, a program that enables DHS to prescreen 100 percent of passengers on flights flying to, from, or within the United States against government watchlists. DHS has also increased enrollment in its trusted traveler programs—which expedite travel for members who pass rigorous, recurrent security checks— to over one million members. With support from international partners and the aviation industry, DHS has implemented pre-departure programs for U.S. bound flights as well as enhanced security measures to strengthen the safety and security of all passengers. These new measures, which cover 100 percent of passengers traveling by air to the United States, utilize real-time, threat-based intelligence along with multiple layers of security, both seen and unseen, to more effectively mitigate evolving terrorist threats.

Pre-Departure Identification

DHS has worked closely with the intelligence and law enforcement communities to develop new mechanisms that identify high-risk travelers prior to departure. The U.S. Government has reformed the criteria and nomination processes for the terrorist watchlist and enhanced its information sharing capabilities to more comprehensively connect available pieces of intelligence to identify individuals who are known to be of security concern as well as people and connections that would otherwise remain unknown. Collectively, these enhancements help prevent dangerous individuals from entering the United States and support enforcement efforts if derogatory information develops after an individual of concern has already been admitted.

The U.S. Government reviews travelers' identity information and travel practices through five reinforcing systems:

- The visa application process, through which DHS provides support to DOS;

---

[7] 9/11 Commission Report, pg. 393

[8] 9/11 Commission Report, pg. 385

- ESTA, which determines eligibility of a person for travel under the VWP;

- The API System, which allows CBP to compare the traveler manifest of commercial and private aircraft, as well as commercial vessels, against law enforcement databases, including the Terrorist Screening Database (TSDB);

- Passenger Name Records (PNR) data, which analyzes information from the carriers' reservation systems to detect links to known or suspected terrorists or patterns of criminal or terrorist activity; and

- Secure Flight, which compares passenger information against government watchlists.

Improved Analysis of Travel-Related Data

While watchlists existed prior to 9/11, they were neither coordinated nor consolidated to the degree and depth commensurate with what exists today. Today, four centers across the federal government provide information regarding potential terrorist travel: TSC, NCTC, the National Targeting Center, and the Human Smuggling and Trafficking Center, all of whom work together, leveraging threat-related intelligence and travel-related data which is essential in identifying, targeting, and interdicting known and suspected terrorists as well as suspicious cargo prior to entering the United States or boarding a flight bound for the United States. In addition, watchlist data that previously had been retained at entry points in the United States has now been pushed overseas, so that suspect travelers do not board an airplane for the U.S. without, at a minimum, additional screening. In fiscal year 2010, DHS identified more than 1,500 passengers on watchlists who had booked international flights. These passengers were denied boarding, received enhanced security screening, or were removed from the watchlists after it was determined that they did not pose a threat.

Visa Waiver Program/ Electronic System for Travel Authorization

VWP enables nationals of 36 participating countries to travel to the United States for stays of 90 days or less without obtaining a visa. Prior to 9/11, there was no advance screening of passengers seeking admission under the VWP. In 2008, DHS implemented ESTA to screen prospective VWP travelers against several databases, including the terrorist watchlist; lost and stolen passports; visa revocations; previous VWP refusals; and public health records. Since January 2009, nationals from all VWP countries, regardless of their port of embarkation, have been required to obtain an approved travel authorization via ESTA prior to boarding a carrier to travel by air or sea to the United States under the VWP.

DHS—in cooperation with DOS and DOJ—has made substantial progress in bringing VWP countries into compliance with the information sharing requirements of the 9/11 Act. The 9/11 Act requires VWP countries to enter into an agreement with the United States to report, or make available to the United States, lost and stolen passport data so that it can be screened against INTERPOL's Stolen and Lost Travel Document database, which contains lost and stolen passport records of more than 150 countries. This requirement has contributed to the overall decline of fraudulent VWP passport intercepts at the border, from 712 in FY2004 to 36 in FY2010.

Visa Security

Through the Visa Security Program (VSP), with DOS concurrence, ICE deploys trained special agents overseas to high-risk visa activity posts in order to identify potential terrorist and criminal threats before they reach the United States. ICE special agents conduct targeted, in-depth reviews of individual visa applications and applicants prior to issuance, and make recommendations to consular officers regarding refusal or revocation of applications when warranted. The VSP is currently deployed to 19 posts in 15 countries.

DHS has also worked closely with federal partners to improve and expand procedures for vetting immigrant and nonimmigrant visa applicants, asylees, and refugees. The interagency vetting process in place today is more robust and considers a far broader range of information than it did in past years. Visa applicants, those seeking to enter the U.S. at a port of entry, refugee, and asylum applicants are subject to rigorous background vetting, biographic and biometric checks— including checks against records obtained by the Department of Defense (DOD) in Iraq and Afghanistan. These enhancements are a reflection of the commitment of DHS and other agencies to conduct the most thorough checks possible to prevent dangerous individuals from gaining access to the United States through the immigration process.

Since March 2010, CBP has utilized their Advanced Targeting System (ATS) platform in partnership with DOS to conduct recurrent vetting of approved visa applications. CBP utilizes ATS to recurrently vet the approved visa applications against the TSDB and other government watchlists. Since the program was implemented, CBP has referred over 1,200 recurrent vetting matches to DOS resulting in over 1,000 visa revocations.

Advance Passenger Information and Passenger Name Records

To identify high-risk travelers and facilitate legitimate travel, DHS requires airlines flying to the United States from foreign countries to provide API, which includes basic information such as name, date of birth, citizenship/nationality and passport number, and PNR, which includes information that travelers provide to airlines when booking their flights, such as itinerary, address, and check-in information, up to 72 hours prior to departure. Since the creation of the Department, DHS has improved its ability to use this and other information to target and identify both known and unknown individuals that are either a threat to aviation or the United States, and to prevent them from either flying to or entering the United States.

During 2008 and 2009, PNR helped the United States identify individuals with potential ties to terrorism in more than 3,000 cases, and in fiscal year 2010, approximately one quarter of those individuals denied entry to the United States for having ties to terrorism were initially identified through the analysis of PNR. PNR analysis also played a critical role in the investigations of Najibullah Zazi, who pled guilty to plotting to bomb New York subways; David Headley, who pled guilty for his role in the 2008 Mumbai terrorist attacks and was suspected of planning attacks in Europe; and Faisal Shahzad, who pled guilty in the 2010 bombing attempt against Times Square in New York.

DHS and the European Union (EU) are completing a new U.S.-EU PNR agreement that improves the privacy protection and security benefits of the 2007 U.S.-EU PNR Agreement currently in effect. The new PNR Agreement, which requires approval by the Council of the European Union and ratification by the European Parliament, will underscore the United States and the European Union's continuing commitment to combat terrorism and serious transnational crime, while respecting privacy.

Secure Flight

Fulfilling a key 9/11 Commission recommendation, DHS fully implemented Secure Flight in November 2010. Under Secure Flight, DHS prescreens 100 percent of passengers on flights flying to, from, or within the United States against government watchlists using passenger names, dates of birth, gender and, if applicable, redress numbers before travelers receive their boarding passes. In addition to facilitating secure travel for all passengers, this program helps prevent the misidentification of passengers who have names similar to individuals on government watchlists. Prior to Secure Flight, airlines were responsible for checking passengers against watchlists. Through Secure Flight, TSA now vets over 14 million passengers weekly.

In addition to facilitating secure travel for all passengers, this program helps prevent the misidentification of passengers who have names similar to individuals on government watchlists and provides the consistent application of an integrated redress process for misidentified individuals through the Department of Homeland Security's Travel Redress Inquiry Program (DHS TRIP). Launched in 2007, DHS TRIP provides a single point of contact for individuals who have inquiries or seek resolution regarding difficulties experienced during travel screening at transportation hubs or crossing U.S. borders.

Pre-Departure Program

Complementing these efforts, CBP has strengthened its in-bound targeting operations to enable CBP to identify high-risk travelers who are likely to be inadmissible into the United States and to recommend to commercial carriers with direct flights to the United States that those individuals not be permitted to board a commercial aircraft through its Pre-Departure program. Since the inception of the Pre-Departure program 2010, CBP has identified over 2,800 passengers who would likely have been found inadmissible upon arrival to the United States.

Pre-clearance Agreements

Pre-clearance agreements are in place with Aruba, Bahamas, Bermuda, Canada and Ireland, allowing DHS to screen travelers and their baggage before takeoff through the same process a traveler would undergo upon arrival at a U.S. port of entry to better target and prevent threats while streamlining legitimate travel. In fiscal year 2010, CBP Officers identified more than 250 positive TSDB matches at pre-clearance locations attempting to travel to the United States. Through collaboration with foreign law enforcement partners, DHS was able to conduct interviews of these individuals, recommend additional screening, and when appropriate, refuse admissions to the U.S. Pre-clearance supports the Department's overall risk-based strategy to identify potential threats prior to travel, while expediting processing at arrival ports of entry.

Immigration Advisory Program

DHS currently has eight Immigration Advisory Program arrangements in six countries, which enable CBP officers posted at foreign airports to use advanced targeting and passenger analysis information to identify high-risk travelers at foreign airports before they board U.S.-bound flights. This program has enabled CBP Officers to identify positive TSDB matches, recommend additional screening, and when appropriate, notify the air carrier that the individual would likely be refused admissions to the U.S.

Trusted Traveler Programs and Enhancing the Traveling Experience

In order to facilitate legitimate travel and effectively deploy screening and security resources, CBP has increased enrollment in its trusted traveler programs from approximately 80,000 members in 2003 to over one million today. CBP currently manages three Trusted Traveler Programs for the passenger environment: NEXUS, the Secure Electronic Network for Travelers Rapid Inspection, and Global Entry, and plans to offer a single application for all modes of travel in the near future. These programs expedite travel for members who voluntarily apply, pay a fee, provide biometric identification, pass a rigorous background check, and undergo recurrent security checks.

In July 2011, TSA released details on a plan to conduct a pilot program in the coming months to enhance TSA's identity-based, pre-flight screening capabilities and provide trusted travelers with expedited screening. During the first phase of testing, certain frequent fliers and all members of CBP's Trusted Traveler programs who are U.S. citizens will be eligible to participate in this pilot, which could qualify them for expedited screening at select checkpoints at certain airports.

DHS is also currently piloting a number of programs to expedite and enhance the traveling experience, including "OneStop," which is designed to reduce wait times by designating primary inspection lanes for international travelers arriving without checked baggage, "Express Connection," which designates customs lanes for travelers who have short time windows between connecting flights, and the Model Ports Initiative, which, in partnership with the private sector, is working to improve the arrival experience at our top 20 international airports.

Risk-Based Screening Strategy for the Future

Recognizing that security screening needs to be constantly updated to address evolving threats, the Administration continues to focus on the implementation of risk-based measures to strengthen aviation security while improving the passenger experience wherever possible. TSA is currently working on a variety of identity-based screening measures that would enable travelers to volunteer more information about themselves prior to flying in order to expedite screening. This is an ongoing, collaborative effort with law enforcement, airport authorities, the aviation industry, and the traveling public. As risk-based screening evolves, DHS and TSA will continue to incorporate random security steps as well as other measures both seen and unseen in order to maintain the safest and most efficient system for the traveling public.

Enhancing Screening for Explosives

RECOMMENDATION: Improve aviation security through enhanced explosive screening[9]

In March 2002, TSA's first cadre of federal screeners included 80 individuals; today more than 52,000 Transportation Security Officers (TSOs), Transportation Security Inspectors, and Behavior Detection Officers serve on the frontlines at more than 450 U.S. airports. Through the Recovery Act and annual appropriations, TSA has accelerated the deployment of new technologies to detect the next generation of threats, including Advanced Imaging Technology (AIT) units, Explosive Detection Systems (EDS), Explosives Trace Detection (ETD) units, Advanced Technology (AT) X-Ray systems, and Bottled Liquid Scanners. Prior to 9/11, limited federal security requirements existed for cargo and baggage screening. Today, 100 percent of all checked and carry-on baggage is screened for explosives and TSA continually assesses intelligence to develop countermeasures in order to enhance its multiple layers of security at airports and onboard aircraft.

Enhanced Screening Technologies

Advanced Imaging Technology

TSA began deploying AIT units in 2008, leading to the detection of hundreds of prohibited, illegal or dangerous items at checkpoints nationwide. AIT safely screens passengers for metallic and non-metallic threats, including weapons, explosives and other objects concealed under layers of clothing. AIT has been evaluated and determined to be safe for all passengers by the Food and Drug Administration, National Institute for Standards and Technology and Johns Hopkins University Applied Physics Laboratory. TSA ensures passenger privacy through the anonymity of AIT images—a privacy filter is applied to blur facial images; all images examined by TSA at airports are permanently deleted immediately once viewed and are not stored, transmitted or printed; and the officer viewing the image never sees the passenger and the officer assisting the passenger cannot view the image. TSA has begun installing new software on millimeter wave AIT units that automatically detect potential threats using a generic outline of a person for all passengers—further enhancing the privacy protections in place for AIT screening.

While TSA does not conduct passenger screening abroad, it requires airports that serve as the last point of departure to the U.S. to meet stringent security standards. To date, several countries—including Canada, Germany, Korea, the Netherlands, Nigeria, Poland, Russia, Ukraine, and the United Kingdom—have deployed or piloted AIT units in their major airports.

---

[9] 9/11 Commission Report, pg. 393

Explosives Trace Detection

ETD units are used by TSOs to screen carry-on articles, checked baggage, and passengers for explosive residue. A swab is used to collect samples, which are electronically analyzed for traces of explosive residue or vapor.

Advanced Technology X-Ray

AT X-Ray machines scan carry-on baggage from multiple angles, providing the operator with a clear image regardless of the bag's orientation within the machine.

Bottled Liquid Scanners

Bottled Liquid Scanners are hand-held or bench-top devices which are capable of detecting explosives and flammable liquids.

Explosive Detection Systems

TSA screens 100 percent of all checked baggage for explosives. Through a sophisticated analysis of each checked bag, EDS can quickly determine if a bag contains a potential threat.

Canines

TSA deploys canine teams to screen air cargo at the nation's highest cargo volume airports and provide explosives detection capabilities in the aviation, mass transit, and maritime transportation sectors. The TSA National Explosive Detection Canine Team Program has grown from 200 in 2001 to 900 teams in 2011. TSA has also developed a Passenger Screening Canine training program to enhance a canine's ability to detect explosive materials in baggage as well as on passengers

Cargo Security

Screening

Prior to 9/11, no federal security requirements existed for cargo screening. Now, 100 percent of all cargo transported on passenger aircraft that depart U.S. airports is screened commensurate with screening of passenger checked baggage. This was accomplished largely through the Certified Cargo Screening Program, which permits entities that have undergone rigorous inspection and certification processes throughout the air cargo supply chain to screen cargo.

In December 2010, TSA implemented requirements for 100 percent screening of high-risk cargo on international flights bound for the United States. Following this, Secretary Napolitano and TSA Administrator Pistole solicited feedback from passenger carriers on their ability to screen 100 percent of all air cargo on international inbound passenger aircraft. The Department is currently evaluating formal industry comment to this proposal in order to finalize its strategy and timeline for implementing the 100 percent international inbound cargo screening requirement. As part of this effort, TSA will work with industry to leverage and enhance ongoing programs such as TSA's National Cargo Security Program recognition process, which certifies foreign aviation security programs that are commensurate with TSA standards.

Global Supply Chain Security

In January 2011, Secretary Napolitano announced a new partnership with the WCO to enlist other nations, international bodies and the private sector in increasing the security of the global supply chain—outlining a series of new initiatives to make the system stronger, smarter and more resilient. The three main elements of this international effort to strengthen the security of the global supply chain include:

- Preventing terrorists from exploiting the global supply chain to plan and execute attacks;

- Protecting the most critical elements of the supply chain system, such as transportation hubs and related critical infrastructure, from attacks and disruptions; and

- Building the resilience of the global supply chain to ensure that if something does happen, the supply chain can recover quickly.

As part of the effort to strengthen the global supply chain, ICE, in coordination with the WCO, launched Operation Global Shield in 2010, a multilateral law enforcement effort aimed at combating the illicit cross-border diversion and trafficking of precursor chemicals for making improvised explosive devices (IED) by monitoring their cross-border movements. In March 2011, the WCO voted to make Project Global Shield a permanent program.

Additionally, the Customs Trade Partnership Against Terrorism (C-TPAT), a voluntary public-private sector partnership program, strengthens cargo security throughout the international supply chain by working closely with importers, carriers, consolidators, licensed customs brokers, and manufacturers. The C-TPAT program—launched in November 2001 with seven participating companies—evaluates trusted shippers through security checks and on site evaluations. As of May 2011, C-TPAT had more than 10,100 Certified Partners worldwide and has conducted more than 17,700 on site validations of manufacturing and logistics facilities in 97 countries, representing some of the highest risk areas of the world.

Strengthening Efforts to Detect and Report Biological, Radiological and Nuclear Threats

RECOMMENDATION: Strengthen counterproliferation efforts to prevent radiological/nuclear terrorism[10]

Countering nuclear, biological, and radiological threats requires a coordinated, whole-of-government approach. The Domestic Nuclear Detection Office (DNDO)—formed in 2005 as part of DHS—works in partnership with agencies across federal, state and local government to prevent and deter attacks using nuclear and radiological weapons through nuclear detection and forensics programs and activities. The Office of Health Affairs (OHA) coordinates the Department's biological and chemical defense activities, providing medical and scientific expertise to support preparedness and response efforts.

Nuclear Detection

DNDO works to improve the nation's capability to detect and report unauthorized attempts to import, develop, or transport nuclear or radiological material for use against the U.S.

Working with partners from across the Administration, including DOD, DOS, Department of Energy, and DOJ, the intelligence community, and the Nuclear Regulatory Commission, DNDO helps integrate interagency efforts to develop nuclear detection capabilities, respond to detection alarms, conduct research and development, and coordinate the development of the global nuclear detection architecture (GNDA). In December 2010, DNDO submitted to Congress the GNDA Strategic Plan, an interagency product designed to guide the nation's nuclear terrorism detection capacity and capability development over the next five years.

DNDO develops nuclear detection capabilities and implements the domestic portion of the GNDA in coordination with federal, state, local, international, and private sector partners as well as the Department's operational components. For example, DNDO has worked with CBP to deploy Radiation Portal Monitors and other radiation detection technologies to seaports, land border ports, and mail facilities around the world. When the Department was formed in 2003, these systems scanned only 68 percent of arriving trucks and passenger vehicles along the Northern border. No systems were deployed to the Southwest border and only one was deployed to a seaport. Today, these systems scan 100 percent of all containerized cargo and personal vehicles arriving in the U.S. through land ports of entry, as well as over 99 percent of arriving sea containers. Additionally, DHS has procured thousands of Personal Radiation Detectors, Radiological Isotope Identification devices, and backpack detectors for CBP, USCG, TSA, and state and local law enforcement across the country to scan cars, trucks, and other items and conveyances

---

[10] 9/11 Commission Report, pg. 381

for the presence of radiological and nuclear materials. DNDO has also made radiological and nuclear detection training available to over 15,000 state and local officers and first responders.

In its fiscal year 2012 budget request, DHS proposed expanding the Securing the Cities (STC) initiative, designed to enhance the nation's ability to detect and prevent a radiological or nuclear attack in the highest risk cities, to include additional urban areas while continuing to support efforts in New York. Through STC, nearly 11,000 personnel in the New York City region have been trained in preventive radiological and nuclear detection operations and nearly 6,000 pieces of radiological detection equipment have been deployed. In April 2011, DNDO and the New York Police Department sponsored a full-scale exercise for radiological and nuclear detection capabilities in the New York City region to assess the ability of STC partners to detect radiological and nuclear materials and deploy personnel, equipment and special units in accordance with established protocols and in response to threat-based intelligence.

To fulfill its mandate to develop, acquire, and support the deployment of radiological and nuclear detection technologies, DNDO has embarked on ambitious research and development programs. Since its inception, DNDO has initiated more than 250 research and development projects with national laboratory, academic, and industrial partners to advance detection technologies. DNDO has also conducted more than 50 test and evaluation campaigns of detection equipment, which have informed federal, state, and local users of the technical and operational performance of various radiological and nuclear detection systems.

Nuclear Forensics

DHS is also responsible for advancing the nation's nuclear forensics capability which, in conjunction with law enforcement and intelligence information, supports the identification of individuals involved in planned or actual attacks using radiological or nuclear weapons or materials.

In fiscal year 2008, DNDO launched the National Nuclear Forensics Expertise Development (NNFED) Program—a collaborative effort with DOE and DOD to address the critical human capital needs of the technical nuclear forensics community. Through NNFED, DNDO supports nuclear forensic education through graduate study and faculty development in the field.

In February 2010, President Obama signed the *Nuclear Forensics and Attribution Act*, which established the National Technical Nuclear Forensics Center (NTNFC) within DNDO to coordinate centralized planning and exercises; provide continual assessment and evaluation; and promote international collaboration. The NTNFC has facilitated assessments of national nuclear forensics capabilities through collaboration with the National Academy of Sciences.

In April 2010, President Obama signed and sent to Congress the *National Strategic Five-Year Plan for Improving the Nuclear Forensics and Attribution Capabilities of the United States*. This strategic plan—developed by DNDO in collaboration with its interagency partners—outlines policy, analytical, and budgetary investments to support and improve the nation's nuclear forensics and attribution capabilities.

Counter-Proliferation

One of DHS's highest priorities is to prevent terrorist groups and hostile nations from illegally obtaining U.S. military products and sensitive technology, including components of weapons of mass destruction. ICE's Counter-Proliferation Investigations program is responsible for overseeing a broad range of investigative activities related to such violations, including the enforcement of U.S. laws involving the export of military items and controlled dual-use goods, as well as exports to sanctioned or embargoed countries.

ICE established the National Export Enforcement Coordination Network to better coordinate export enforcement efforts among law enforcement agencies and with the intelligence community. In addition, through Project Shield America, ICE conducts outreach to manufacturers and exporters of strategic commodities that are believed to be targeted for procurement by terrorist organizations and the countries that support them, as well as countries identified as weapons proliferators. In November 2010, President Obama issued an Executive Order authorizing the establishment of the Export Enforcement Coordination Center to coordinate and enhance export control enforcement efforts among federal law enforcement agencies, export licensing agencies, and the intelligence community. The center will begin operations in late 2011.

Nuclear/Radiological Preparedness and Response

Through the Federal Radiological Emergency Preparedness Coordination Committee, as part of the National Response Framework, FEMA provides detailed information regarding roles, responsibilities, and coordinating instructions for a range of radiological and nuclear threats to planners across all levels of government, the private sector, and non-governmental organizations. Recently, FEMA and the Nuclear Regulatory Commission have updated the Radiological Emergency Preparedness Program to focus on planning and preparedness for threats that could affect the nation's commercial nuclear power plants.

Preparing for and Protecting Against Biological Threats

Since the anthrax attacks 10 years ago, the Department has made great strides in protecting the nation from, and preparing federal, state, and local governments to respond to biological attacks.

In 2003, the Department stood up the BioWatch system—a federally-managed, locally-operated, nationwide bio-surveillance system designed to detect the intentional release of aerosolized biological agents which is currently operational in approximately 30 cities and states. In 2010, the Department began testing the next generation of automated early detection systems, known as Gen-3, which is expected to significantly reduce the time between a release of a biothreat agent and confirmation of that release.

To improve state and local biopreparedness, the Department established the first formalized sharing of public health and intelligence information with state and local health partners in 2009. In 2010, the Department developed and conducted a series of biodefense response exercises, including one in each of the 10 FEMA regions, involving more than 1,000 state and local officials. The Department has also contributed to the physical safety and security of biological select agent facilities by completing Buffer Zone Plans and Site Assistance Visits, and providing grant funding to first responders at these facilities.

Recognizing the critical need to dispense life-saving medical countermeasures to those potentially exposed to aerosolized anthrax spores within 48 hours of exposure, the Department's Office of Health Affairs developed a concept of operations for a rapid federal response to support state and local jurisdiction plans. Additionally, DHS stood up a program that ensures the Department's mission essential functions by distributing medical countermeasures to personnel serving in critical roles during an emergency.

Protecting Cyber Networks and Critical Physical Infrastructure

RECOMMENDATION: Assess critical infrastructure and readiness[11]

Over the past ten years, DHS has made significant strides in enhancing the security of the nation's critical physical infrastructure as well as its cyber infrastructure and networks. Key tools include the National Cybersecurity Protection System (NCPS) – of which the EINSTEIN cyber intrusion detection system is a key component – and the National Cybersecurity and Communications Integration Center (NCCIC), a DHS-led coordinated watch and warning center that serves as the nation's principal hub for organizing cyber response efforts. In addition, DHS and DOD signed a landmark memorandum of agreement to align and enhance America's capabilities to protect against threats to critical civilian and military computer systems and networks. Further, DHS led the effort to develop the National Infrastructure Protection Plan (NIPP), a comprehensive risk management framework for all levels of government, private industry, nongovernmental entities and tribal partners, while implementing the Chemical Facility Anti-Terrorism Standards (CFATS) to regulate security at high-risk chemical facilities. In addition, DHS conducts comprehensive risk-based security, vulnerability and capability assessments of critical infrastructures, provides technical assistance and grant funding to bolster local capabilities, and facilitates information sharing with key sectors.

Safeguarding Cyber Infrastructure and Networks

The rapid and dispersed rate of change in the cyber sphere presents many challenges. The rising volume and virulence of attacks have the potential to degrade economic capacity and threaten basic services. Today's threats to cybersecurity require the engagement of the entire society—from government and law enforcement to the private sector and importantly, members of the public—to block malicious actors while bolstering defensive capabilities.

DHS is responsible for protecting the federal executive branch civilian agencies and guiding the protection of the nation's critical infrastructure and connections to cyberspace. This includes the "dot-gov" world, where the government maintains essential functions that provide services to the American people as well as the systems and networks that support the financial services, energy, and defense industries.

---

[11] 9/11 Commission Report, pg. 428

Collaboration with Public and Private Sectors

In October 2010, Secretary Napolitano and Secretary of Defense Robert Gates signed a Memorandum of Agreement to align and enhance America's capabilities to protect against threats to critical civilian and military computer systems and networks. The Agreement embeds DOD cyber analysts within DHS and sends DHS privacy, civil liberties, and legal personnel to DOD's National Security Agency to strengthen the nation's cybersecurity posture and ensure the protection of fundamental rights.

In November 2010, the Multi-State Information Sharing and Analysis Center, funded in part by DHS, opened the Cyber Security Operations Center, a 24-hour watch and warning facility, to enhance situational awareness at the state and local level and allow the federal government to quickly and efficiently provide critical cyber risk, vulnerability, and mitigation data to state and local governments.

In partnership with the private sector, the U.S. Computer Emergency Readiness Team (US-CERT) takes proactive measures to stop possible threats from reaching an even broader audience by developing and sharing standardized threat indication, prevention, mitigation, and response information products with its "dot-gov" partners. In addition, US-CERT hosts the Joint Agency Cyber Knowledge Exchange Program, an analyst-to-analyst information sharing forum between US-CERT and the rest of the federal government for the exchange of classified and unclassified cyber threat information and techniques for mitigating and defending against cyber threats.

Protecting Critical Infrastructure and Its Connections to Cyberspace

Protecting critical infrastructure and its connections to cyberspace—including the systems and networks that support the financial services, energy, and defense industries— requires a full range of partners, including other government agencies, the private sector and individuals

DHS developed the first-ever National Cyber Incident Response Plan in September 2010 to coordinate the response of multiple federal agencies, state and local governments, and hundreds of private firms, to incidents at all levels. DHS tested this plan during the CyberStorm III national exercise, which simulated a large-scale attack on the nation's critical information infrastructure and included participation from seven cabinet agencies, 11 states, 12 international partners, and 60 private sector companies.

DHS also works with the private sector, other government agencies and the international community every day to mitigate risks by leveraging the tools, tradecraft, and techniques malicious actors use and converting them into actionable information for all 18 critical infrastructure sectors to use against cyber threats. In October 2009, DHS opened the new NCCIC—a 24-hour, DHS-led coordinated watch and warning center to serve as the nation's principal hub for organizing cyber response efforts and maintaining the national cyber and communications common operational picture. DHS also implemented the Cybersecurity Partners Local Access Plan, which allows security-cleared owners and operators of critical infrastructure and key resources, as well as state technology officials and law enforcement officials, to access secret-level cybersecurity information via local fusion centers.

Protecting the "dot-gov" World

In close partnership with other federal agencies and the private sector, DHS utilizes NCPS, of which the EINSTEIN intrusion detection system is a key component, to protect the dot-gov domains. The EINSTEIN system, initially deployed in 2004, helps block malicious actors from accessing federal executive branch civilian agencies, while working closely with those agencies to bolster their defensive capabilities. Recently, DHS deployed EINSTEIN 2—an automated cyber surveillance system that monitors federal internet traffic for malicious intrusions—at 15 Departments and agencies and four Managed Trusted Internet Protocol Service providers. At full operational capability, EINSTEIN 3 will provide DHS with the ability to detect malicious activity and disable attempted intrusions automatically, a significant improvement in the Department's ability to prevent cyber intrusions on federal executive branch civilian networks and systems. Once fully deployed, EINSTEIN 2 and EINSTEIN 3 will provide cyber protection capabilities to more than 110 federal civilian executive branch departments and agencies.

Additionally, as part of the Comprehensive National Cybersecurity Initiative, DHS works to reduce and consolidate the number of external connections that federal agencies have to the Internet through the Trusted Internet Connection (TIC) initiative. This initiative reduces the number of potential vulnerabilities to government networks and allows DHS to focus monitoring efforts and security capabilities on limited and known avenues for Internet traffic.

Intelligence and Cybersecurity

The DHS I&A works with the National Protection and Programs Directorate (NPPD) to monitor and report on threats and intrusions to federal government departments, as well as state and local governments. By embedding intelligence analysts at US-CERT, the Industrial Control Systems Cyber Emergency Response Team and the NCCIC, I&A is able to analyze intrusion detection information gathered from DHS sensors like EINSTEIN as well as investigative information from DHS components to provide a national intelligence perspective to cyber incidents. Analysis is then shared with the federal, state, local and tribal government agencies in the form of Homeland Intelligence Reports.

Additionally, I&A integrates all-source intelligence from the intelligence community with information provided by private sector owners and operators of CIKR to provide a more comprehensive tactical and strategic understanding of cyber threats. I&A disseminates this information through regular intelligence products and briefings to the private sector.

World-class Cybersecurity Professionals

DHS is building a world-class cybersecurity team by hiring a diverse group of cybersecurity professionals—computer engineers, scientists, and analysts—to secure the nation's digital assets and protect against cyber threats to CIKR. Through its Cybersecurity Workforce Initiative, DHS has increased its cyber staff by 500 percent while working with universities to build the cybersecurity pipeline through competitive scholarship, fellowship, and internship programs to continue to attract top talent.

Research and Development

S&T is leading the federal government's efforts to develop and deploy secure internet protocols that protect consumers and industry. Major companies throughout the cyber industry are now using DHS's protocols in their products to better secure their corporate and global infrastructure. S&T is also supporting efforts to protect internet infrastructure from attack by creating new tools to detect malicious software on networks and new test beds and measurement techniques to help develop countermeasures for current and emerging cyber attacks.

Building Public Awareness

DHS is also committed to increasing public awareness about cybersecurity and empowering individuals and enterprises across cyber networks to enhance their own security operations. In 2010, the Department launched the *"Stop. Think. Connect."* public cybersecurity awareness campaign to increase public understanding of cyber threats and promote simple steps the public can take to increase their safety and security online.

Infrastructure Protection

Since fiscal year 2006, DHS has provided more than $3.6 billion in grant funding through the Port Security, Transit Security and Buffer Zone Protection grant programs to protect critical infrastructure from terrorism. These grants support security plans, facility security upgrades, training, exercises, law enforcement anti-terrorism operations, and capital projects for risk mitigation of high threat infrastructure.

Risk-Based Infrastructure Protection Plans and Standards

The first NIPP was published in 2006 as a comprehensive risk management framework to define critical infrastructure protection roles and responsibilities for all levels of government, private industry, and nongovernmental entities. In 2009, DHS revised the NIPP to integrate resilience and protection and broaden the focus of NIPP-related programs and activities to an all-hazards environment. DHS also developed an annual National Risk Profile that provides a multi-hazard assessment of risks facing critical infrastructure, including terrorist threats, cyber risks, and natural disasters.

Since 2007, DHS has implemented the CFATS to regulate security at high-risk chemical facilities. To date, the Department has reviewed an estimated 40,000 consequence assessment questionnaires submitted by potentially high-risk chemical facilities. Of these, approximately 4,500 facilities have been preliminarily identified as high-risk, resulting in the development and submission of Security Vulnerability Assessments. Of those facilities, nearly all have received final high-risk determinations and are in the process of completing Site Security Plans to bolster safety and security measures.

Risk-Based Assessments and Information Sharing

The Department's Office of Infrastructure Protection (IP) has conducted more than 1,900 security surveys and more than 2,500 vulnerability assessments of the nation's critical infrastructure to identify security gaps and potential vulnerabilities and provide protective measures recommendations to enhance the protection and resilience of the nation's critical infrastructure. IP has also conducted more than 1,400 capability assessments of state and local bomb squads, explosives detection canine teams, dive teams, and SWAT teams to identify potential gaps and provide recommendations to mitigate vulnerabilities.

In order to enhance local capabilities, IP conducts Regional Resiliency Assessment Programs on clusters of high consequence critical infrastructure to coordinate protection efforts in major metropolitan areas. IP has also worked with state and local partners to develop 20 Multi-Jurisdiction IED Security Plans for high-risk urban areas that outline specific bombing prevention actions that reduce vulnerabilities and mitigate the risk of IED attacks.

USCG's MSRAM has been used to assess over 28,000 potential terrorist targets, spanning all 18 critical infrastructure sectors, including waterside commercial nuclear facilities. Under the Maritime Transportation Security Act, maritime CIKR are required to have facility security plans which the USCG must approve.

The Federal Protective Service also provides risk assessment and mitigation, physical security, and federal law enforcement training and oversight to enhance protection at more than 9,000 federally owned and leased facilities in all 50 states and the U.S. territories.

Since 2006, the Critical Infrastructure Key Resources Information Sharing Environment (CIKR ISE) has provided over 13,000 products, reaching over 40,000 federal, state, local, territorial, tribal and private sector partners. The CIKR ISE also provides the private sector entry into NSI through the SAR Reporting Tool for Critical Infrastructure, and is a mechanism for fusion centers to share regional infrastructure protection information directly with their private sector partners via the Homeland Security Information Network-Critical Sectors.

Protective Security Advisors

The Department has deployed Protective Security Advisors (PSAs) to all 50 states, Puerto Rico, and the District of Columbia to support state, local, tribal and territorial officials and the private sector with critical infrastructure security efforts; coordinate and conduct vulnerability assessments and training; respond to all hazard incidents impacting critical infrastructure; and support effective information sharing and situational awareness. Because PSAs are strategically dispersed across the United States, they are often the first DHS personnel to respond to incidents that may require federal intervention, especially those involving critical infrastructure.

New Infrastructure Protection Tools

To facilitate the implementation of the NIPP and to support efforts to develop and implement critical infrastructure protection and resilience capabilities, the Department's Office of

Infrastructure Protection has established new technologies and tools for use by DHS and its federal, state, local and private sector partners. These capabilities include:

- *Automated Critical Asset Management System (ACAMS):* ACAMs is a secure, web-based portal developed in partnership with the State, Local, Tribal, Territorial Government Coordinating Council to help local communities build critical infrastructure protection programs in their local jurisdictions and implement the NIPP; and

- *Infrastructure Information Collection System (IICS):* IICS allow users to easily access, search, retrieve, and export infrastructure data contained within disparate IP systems/datasets and other federal, state, and local systems, enabling information sharing across organizations.

The DHS S&T Directorate also conducts research and development to create new technologies to enhance critical infrastructure security. These include:

- *Integrated Rapid Visual Screening Tool for Tunnels and Mass Transit Stations:* Assesses the level of risk for buildings and infrastructure from terrorist attacks and natural disasters and helps design professionals, building owners, and first responders understand the risk and resilience of buildings and infrastructure. The tool is currently used by TSA and local law enforcement agencies;

- *Resilient Tunnel Project:* Develops innovative, feasible, and cost efficient solutions to limit water flow in case of a mass transit tunnel breach and is currently evaluating inflatable tunnel plugs. This project was initiated in 2008 as part of the mass transit risk mitigation partnership led by S&T and TSA in collaboration with the DOT;

- *Blast/Projectile – Protective Measures and Design Tool Project:* Develops mitigation schemes for critical transit infrastructure such as underwater tunnels, transit stations, and ventilation structures as well as towers, cables, suspenders, and other critical bridge components;

- *Bridge Vulnerability Project:* Collects vintage components from long-span bridges and evaluates their vulnerability to an explosive attack in order to refine blast modeling tools;

- *Unified Blast Analysis Tool Project:* Predicts blast pressures in transportation tunnel systems, determining possible structural failures;

- *Geospatial Location Accountability and Navigation Systems for Emergency Responders (GLANSER):* Enables incident commanders to locate and track first responder personnel during an incident through locators, alarms, communications, and visualizations that can be integrated into Personal Protection Equipment; and

- *Controlled Impact Rescue Tool:* Breaches reinforced concrete walls in minutes in order to significantly decrease the time needed to perform urban search and rescue operations. FEMA plans to deploy this tool in support of its Urban Search and Rescue teams in 2011.

Each of these projects involves partnerships with stakeholders from all levels of government in order to complete comprehensive development, testing, and analysis.

Infrastructure Protection Training and Education

DHS has developed a variety of infrastructure protection training and education tools for its partners at the state and local level. In total, more than 35,000 state, local and private sector security partners have taken risk mitigation training on a range of topics. DHS training and education tools include:

- *FEMA Emergency Management Institute (EMI)*, which currently hosts 12 cross-sector and sector-specific training courses in the CIKR curriculum, including a resilience course covering the NIPP;

- *IP Bombing Prevention Training*, which develops awareness of terrorist threats to critical infrastructure among state, local, and private sector partners, and educates participants on strategies for detecting and mitigating these threats. To date, over 35,000 participants have been trained;

- *IP Bomb-making Materials Awareness Training*, which has been offered to over 4,000 local law enforcement personnel;

- *TRIPwire*, an online information-sharing network for bomb squads, law enforcement, and other emergency services personnel, which provides the latest information on terrorist IED tactics, techniques, and procedures to over 11,500 registered users; and

- *Critical Infrastructure Asset Protection Technical Assistance Program*, which is a course designed to assist state and local law enforcement, first responders, emergency management, and other homeland security officials in developing and implementing a comprehensive critical infrastructure protection program in their respective jurisdictions.

In addition to training, DHS is leading a critical infrastructure higher education initiative designed to ensure that critical infrastructure is included as an essential element of homeland security and other relevant degree and certificate programs. This effort, conducted through George Mason University, is designed to help prepare the critical infrastructure protection workforce of the future by developing and sharing core critical infrastructure protection courses across the academic community.

RECOMMENDATION: Allocate homeland security funds based on risk[12]

Since the Department's creation, DHS has awarded more than $31 billion based on risk to build and sustain targeted capabilities and strengthen state and local prevention efforts across the homeland security enterprise.

To support state, local, and tribal governments and the private sector in strengthening preparedness for acts of terrorism, major disasters, and other emergencies, since fiscal year 2003, DHS has awarded more than $31 billion in preparedness grant funding based on risk to build and sustain targeted capabilities to prevent, protect against, respond to, and recover from threats or acts of terrorism.

The highest risk cities in the United States continue to face the most significant threats, and the fiscal year 2011 homeland security grants, which were cut by nearly a quarter from fiscal year 2010, focus the limited resources that were appropriated to prepare for these evolving threats. At the same time, all cities sustain some degree of risk. To address this, Congress created the State Homeland Security Grant Program (SHSGP), which establishes a minimum level of homeland security funding for all states to build preparedness capabilities at the local level. DHS has distributed more than $8 billion in SHSGP grants since 2003.

DHS continues to focus grant funding on realizing and sustaining operational priorities. For example, the fiscal year 2011 Urban Areas Security Initiative (UASI) grants encourage the development and sustainment of baseline capabilities at fusion centers. Further, to address homegrown extremism, DHS has prioritized grant-funded prevention activities that directly support local homeland security efforts to understand, recognize, prepare for, prevent and respond to pre-operational activity and other crimes that are precursors or indicators of terrorist activity, in accordance with privacy, civil rights and civil liberties protections.

---

[12] 9/11 Commission Report, pg. 396

RECOMMENDATION: Track and disrupt terrorist financing[13]

Since 9/11, DHS has significantly expanded its ability to track and disrupt terrorist financing, through the expansion of USSS's Electronic Crimes Task Force (ECTF) program as well as ICE and CBP initiatives to combat bulk cash smuggling.

Disrupting terrorist financing is one of a number of tools that the U.S. Government employs to counter terrorism. USSS has expanded its ECTF program from seven in 2001 to more than thirty domestic and international task forces today. These task forces are designed to prevent, detect, and investigate various forms of electronic crimes, including potential terrorist attacks against critical infrastructure and financial payment systems.

ICE has a lead role in combating bulk cash smuggling, a common strategy used by criminals seeking to move illicit proceeds across transnational borders. In August 2009, ICE established the National Bulk Cash Smuggling Center, a 24/7 operations and intelligence facility which supports federal, state, local, and foreign law enforcement efforts to identify, investigate, and disrupt bulk cash smuggling activities throughout the world.

ICE's Operation Firewall, a bulk-cash smuggling initiative focused on intercepting southbound currency smuggling, has led to hundreds of arrests and the seizure of more than $516 million, including $277 million seized overseas. ICE's Cornerstone Outreach Initiative, which focuses on detecting and closing gaps within U.S. financial, trade, and transportation sectors, has resulted in more than 400 criminal investigations that have led to approximately 270 arrests, 230 indictments, more than 180 convictions, and the seizure of nearly $157 million. In addition, ICE has provided outreach and training on the interdiction and investigation of bulk currency violations to more than 2,500 law enforcement, financial, and government officials in more than 85 countries.

CBP efforts to disrupt terrorist financing include approximately 1,500 canine teams strategically stationed throughout the United States. Under the Southwest Border Initiative, DHS began screening 100 percent of southbound rail shipments for illegal weapons, drugs, and cash. In FY 2009 and 2010, CBP seized over $104 million in illegal currency departing the U.S. at ports of entry.

---

[13] 9/11 Commission Report, pg. 382

RECOMMENDATION: Improve interoperable communications at all levels of government[14]

Since 9/11, DHS has implemented strategies to transform and strengthen interoperable communications across the country. Through the establishment of the Office of Emergency Communications, more than $4 billion in dedicated grant funding for state and local interoperability efforts, and the development and deployment of new technologies, DHS has helped to enhance coordination to ensure that emergency response providers can communicate during natural disasters, acts of terrorism, and other catastrophic events. Additionally, in 2011, the Administration announced a plan to deploy a nationwide, interoperable wireless broadband network for public safety.

Enhancing Interoperability through the Office of Emergency Communications

As the Government Accountability Office (GAO) has noted, federal, state, and local governments face several major challenges in addressing interoperability in their wireless communications. Establishing national interoperability performance goals and standards and balancing them with the flexibility needed to address differences in state, regional, and local needs and conditions is complicated. Different first responders each have their own professional practices, public safety missions, emergency response procedures, communication protocols, and radio frequencies. No single group can address interoperability challenges alone; rather, it requires the partnership, leadership, and coordinated planning of everyone involved.

Through the Office of Emergency Communications (OEC), which was established in 2007, DHS has partnered with federal, state, and local stakeholders to identify solutions to emergency communications challenges. In 2008, OEC developed the National Emergency Communications Plan (NECP) in coordination with more than 150 public safety practitioners at all levels of government and across responder disciplines. The NECP serves as the nation's first nationwide strategic plan to improve emergency communications and drive measurable progress at all levels of government.

In 2010, OEC worked with 60 urban areas to assess emergency communications during a real-world situation. All 60 urban areas successfully demonstrated response-level emergency communications. These demonstrations illustrate how the significant organizational and technical investments funded through the Interoperable Emergency Communications and UASI Grants have improved their emergency communications capabilities in recent years.

Perhaps most significantly, in February 2011, President Obama announced the Wireless Innovation and Infrastructure Initiative to develop and deploy a nationwide, interoperable wireless

---

[14] 9/11 Commission Report, pg. 397

broadband network for public safety. OEC supports the deployment of the network by helping to set the broad policy framework and incorporating the views and requirements of the public safety community in broadband network planning and implementation efforts.

In addition, the following accomplishments are a result of DHS efforts to coordinate with stakeholders from the federal, state, and local responder communities as well as the private sector, to improve interoperability:

- *Enhanced Statewide Coordination:* The creation of Statewide Communication Interoperability Plans and appointment of Statewide Interoperability Coordinators has improved coordination of emergency communications activities and investments throughout the states and territories;

- *Common Plans, Protocols, and Procedures:* The development and use of standardized plans, protocols, and procedures has strengthened command, control, and communications among emergency response agencies in the field. OEC and FEMA have worked with more than 140 jurisdictions to develop Tactical Interoperable Communications Plans that document formalized interoperability governance groups, standardized policies and procedures, and emergency communications equipment inventories. In addition, more than 30 states are implementing plain language protocols to simplify and standardize the language used to share information and communicate during an emergency;

- *Targeted Technical Assistance:* As part of the NECP, OEC has implemented a technical assistance strategy to ensure that all states and territories can request and receive emergency communications assistance, while focusing support on states and urban areas most in need;

- *Increased Training Opportunities:* To improve emergency responders' capabilities, OEC has trained more than 3,500 first responders, technicians, and planners to lead communications at incidents across the nation. This training has also contributed to recovery efforts outside of the United States, such as the response to the 2010 earthquake in Haiti; and

- *Improved Governance and Coordination:* OEC has worked with federal, state, local, territorial, and tribal agencies to stand up formal decision-making structures that increase coordination, information sharing, and oversight of interoperability including:

  - Statewide Interoperability Governing Bodies, which include representatives from all levels of government to coordinate and support statewide interoperability;

  - Regional Emergency Communications Coordination Working Groups, which coordinate multi-state emergency communications efforts; and

  - Emergency Communications Preparedness Center, which DHS established in 2009 to be the central federal coordination point for interoperable and operable emergency communications.

DHS Components' Efforts to Increase Interoperability

- *Integrated Public Alert and Warning System:* FEMA is developing the nation's next-generation infrastructure of alert and warning capabilities, which expands upon the traditional audio-only radio and television Emergency Alert System and will provide emergency information to people before, during and after a disaster. The initial operating capability for delivery of alerts to mobile devices will begin in 2011, allowing emergency managers to send geographically-targeted alert and warning messages to citizens. Known as the Commercial Mobile Alert System, or PLAN (Personal Localized Alerting Network), this new public safety system allows customers who own an enabled mobile device to receive geographically-targeted, text-like messages alerting them of imminent threats to safety in their area. In addition, federal, state and local officials will be able to send alerts and warnings to broadcasters through various digital communications paths by 2012.

- *Multi-Band Radio Technology:* S&T is currently testing and evaluating this portable radio technology that enables emergency responders to communicate with partner agencies regardless of the radio band on which they operate.

- *Geospatial Location Accountability and Navigation Systems for Emergency Responders (GLANSER):* Enables incident commanders to locate and track first responder personnel during an incident through locators, alarms, communications, and visualizations that can be integrated into Personal Protection Equipment.

- *Virtual USA:* Launched in 2009, this information-sharing system links disparate tools and technologies at all levels of government to share the location and operational status of critical resources through voice, video, geospatial platforms, and imagery with the homeland security and emergency management community. Virtual USA was used to assist in the response to the BP Deepwater Horizon Oil Spill and was used during the 2011 National Level Exercise (NLE).

- *Watchkeeper Information Sharing System:* USCG is standardizing local maritime port interoperability through the establishment of the Interagency Operations Centers framework at the nation's major ports. This includes the *Watchkeeper Information Sharing System* which facilitates joint operations planning and monitoring at individual ports.

International Interoperability

The Department is working with Mexico and Canada to enhance interoperable communications along and across the Southern and Northern borders in order to ensure that emergency response providers can communicate during natural disasters, acts of terrorism, and other catastrophic events.

The United States and Mexico are establishing a new cross-border communications network, which will improve incident response and coordination among participating federal, state, and local law enforcement and public safety personnel along the border. Installation is scheduled to begin this summer.

U.S. Department of Homeland Security: Implementing 9/11 Commission Recommendations

DHS and Public Safety Canada also work together to enhance cross-border interoperable communications planning, policy development and operations through the annual Canada-U.S. Cross-Border Interoperable Communications Workshops.

In May 2011, DHS awarded $25 million in grant funding under the Border Interoperability Demonstration Project—a one-time competitive grant program focused on developing innovative solutions to strengthen interoperable emergency communications along the U.S. borders with Canada and Mexico.

RECOMMENDATION: Establish a unified incident command system[15]

Since 9/11, DHS has made significant progress in establishing and improving a unified incident command system to respond to a wide range of threats, from natural disasters to coordinated attacks.

The Incident Command System (ICS) provides a flexible mechanism for coordinated and collaborative management for many incidents, covering large or small geographical areas, single or multiple governments, nongovernmental, and/or private sector organizations.

FEMA's disaster response operations are also organized along ICS principles. FEMA has established sixteen Incident Management Assistance Teams (IMATs) that utilize the ICS as their core organizational management structure. Using the authorities outlined under HSPD 5 and the Stafford Act, FEMA leads the federal interagency team in support of state governors. Throughout the devastating multi-state flooding and tornado response operations during the Spring of 2011, FEMA-led teams successfully implemented the National Incident Management System and ICS to achieve fully coordinated interagency and intergovernmental operations to best meet the needs of survivors. FEMA, through the establishment of efficient Unified Coordination Groups in each impacted state, facilitated the integration of all available resources into these complex multi-state, multi-Region events.

As directed by PPD-8, issued in March 2011, DHS is developing a national preparedness system in coordination with partners across the federal government that will include enhanced guidance for planning, organization, equipment, training, and exercises to build and maintain domestic capabilities. The system will provide an all-of-Nation approach for building and sustaining a cycle of preparedness activities over time.

---

[15] 9/11 Commission Report, pg. 397

RECOMMENDATION: Prioritize private sector preparedness[16]

Since 9/11, DHS has prioritized private sector preparedness through programs such as the Voluntary Private Sector Preparedness Accreditation and Certification Program (PS-Prep™), Ready Business, the development and deployment of new technologies, and by incorporating private sector partners from the outset when developing new policies, programs and initiatives.

Private Sector Preparedness

Fulfilling the 9/11 Commission's recommendation to create a program to improve private sector preparedness for disasters and emergencies, in June 2010, DHS announced the adoption of the final standards for PS-Prep™—a partnership between DHS and the private sector that enables private entities to receive emergency preparedness certification. Since PS-Prep™ began, DHS and FEMA have adopted three industry standards to assist organizations in assessing their preparedness and resiliency. IP is currently working with critical infrastructure owners and operators across the 18 CIKR sectors to develop guidance documents that support voluntary participation and further implementation of the PS-Prep™ program.

Private Sector Emergency Response

In 2007, FEMA established a Private Sector Division to facilitate full engagement of the private sector in emergency management. The Division has made it a priority to create tools, initiatives and opportunities to increase preparedness levels and community resilience. In 2010, FEMA deployed staff to focus specifically on private sector outreach in each of FEMA's 10 regions, allowing FEMA to conduct more direct and widespread collaboration with the private sector in coordination with states and other levels of government. More recently, the Private Sector Division and FEMA's National Exercise Division created new opportunities for the private sector to participate in NLE 2011. Over 3,000 organizations participated as a result—a more than 700 percent increase from any previous NLE.

FEMA also continues to promote private sector preparedness through its Ready Business campaign, a nationwide initiative that provides materials to businesses of all sizes to encourage business continuity planning and crisis management. Ready Business is part of larger preparedness outreach efforts by FEMA that include the Ready campaign, Citizen Corps, and National Preparedness Month, held each September to encourage Americans to prepare for emergencies in their homes, businesses, and communities.

---

[16] 9/11 Commission Report, pg. 398

Private Sector Partnerships to Develop and Deploy New Technologies

S&T, through its implementation of the Support Anti-Terrorism by Fostering Effective Technologies (SAFETY) Act of 2002, has incentivized the development and deployment of effective anti-terrorism technologies and services by the private sector throughout the United States. Since the first applications were received in 2004, more than 460 qualified anti-terrorism technologies have been approved. These technologies have been widely deployed to protect commercial facilities, critical infrastructure, transportation hubs, ports, borders, sports venues, and commercial aviation.

S&T also works with the private sector through the System Efficacy through Commercialization, Utilization, Relevance and Evaluation (SECURE) program, which was launched in 2008. Under SECURE, the government provides companies with detailed requirements of a needed technology, product, or service, along with an estimate of the potential market. In exchange, companies use their own funds to perform research and development to meet those requirements. This saves both government and the private sector resources: the government does not spend money on research and development while companies do not waste resources trying to determine on their own what the government ultimately is going to need. Once the technology, product or service is complete and verified through independent third-party testing and evaluation, the technology can be certified as having met the SECURE requirements. The first SECURE certified product—a blast-resistant video system designed by Visual Defence, Inc. that functions similarly to the "black box" found in airplanes—was unveiled in April 2011.

Private Sector Engagement Across DHS Missions

DHS has also partnered with the private sector to strengthen cargo security, cybersecurity, and aviation security as discussed throughout this report. For example, CBP's C-TPAT program is a voluntary public-private sector partnership to strengthen cargo security throughout the international supply chain by working closely with importers, carriers, consolidators, licensed customs brokers, and manufacturers. In December 2010, CBP, TSA, and the air cargo industry launched the Air Cargo Advance Screening Pilot to share electronic shipping information for international flights to the United States prior to departure to improve the identification of high-risk shipments. Further, in 2010, DHS implemented the Cybersecurity Partners Local Access Plan, which allows security-cleared private sector owners and operators of CIKR to access secret-level cybersecurity information and video teleconference calls via local fusion centers.

Moreover, the NCCIC works closely with private sector stakeholders from the various sectors including financial services and critical infrastructure to share valuable threat data and offer support with incident response.

Bolstering the Security of U.S Borders and Identification Documents

RECOMMENDATION: Standardize secure identification[17]

DHS has taken significant steps to strengthen security, reduce fraud and improve the reliability and accuracy of personal identification documents while enhancing privacy safeguards, including fundamentally transforming the way travelers enter the United States from within the Western Hemisphere through implementation of the Western Hemisphere Travel Initiative (WHTI) and from other countries around the world through the Visa Waiver Program, Visa Security Program and US-VISIT biometric identity and verification process .

Western Hemisphere Travel Initiative

In 2009, DHS implemented the Western Hemisphere Travel Initiative (WHTI), a program that strengthens border security for land and sea travel to the U.S., while facilitating legitimate travel and trade by requiring that U.S., Mexican and Canadian citizens present a passport or other secure travel document[18] that denotes identity and citizenship when crossing the border. Prior to the implementation of WHTI, there was no documentary requirement for U.S. or Canadian citizens to enter the United States from within the Western Hemisphere; travelers could present any of numerous documents or simply make an oral declaration without presenting any documentation. In 2005, DHS checked five percent of all passengers crossing land borders by vehicles against law enforcement databases. Today, due to WHTI, the national query rate is over 97 percent.

To support WHTI, DHS has worked with U.S. governors and Canadian government officials to develop state and provincial Enhanced Driver's Licenses (EDL) that denote identity and citizenship for frequent border crossers, and with DOS to develop a wallet-sized U.S. Passport Card. Both documents, as well as others developed for WHTI, can be electronically verified with the issuing agency at the port of entry. CBP and Canada Border Services (CBSA) Agency also worked to expand enrollment in the NEXUS trusted traveler program. The U.S. has deployed Radio Frequency Identification technology readers at ports that cover 99 percent of inbound vehicle traffic at the Northern Border and allows the documents to be read as the traveler is approaching the inspection booth.

CBP is also working with tribes across the country on the development of Enhanced Tribal Cards (ETCs). To date, CBP has signed Memoranda of Agreement for the development of ETCs with the Kootenai Tribe of Idaho, the Pascua Yaqui of Arizona, the Tohono O'Odham of Arizona, the Seneca Nation of New York, the Coquille of Idaho, and the Hydaburg of Alaska.

---

[17] 9/11 Commission Report, pg. 390

[18] WHTI-compliant documents include passports, U.S. passport cards, military identification cards, trusted traveler cards, Enhanced Driver's Licenses, and Enhanced Tribal Cards.

Visa Waiver Program and Lost and Stolen Passport Screening

As discussed in previous sections, the VWP enables nationals of 36 participating countries to travel to the United States for stays of 90 days or less without obtaining a visa. DHS implemented ESTA in 2008 to screen VWP applicants prior to travel to the United States and, as a result, has virtually eliminated the paper arrival/departure form (Form I-94W) for authorized travelers arriving at airports or seaports from nations participating in the VWP.

DHS—in cooperation with DOS and DOJ—has made substantial progress in bringing VWP countries into compliance with the information sharing requirements of the 9/11 Act. The 9/11 Act requires VWP countries to enter into an agreement with the United States to report, or make available to the United States, lost and stolen passport data so that it can be screened against INTERPOL's Stolen and Lost Travel Document database, which contains the lost and stolen passport records of more than 150 countries. To date, 34 of the 36 VWP countries have reached such agreements. This requirement has contributed to the overall decline of fraudulent VWP document intercepts at the border, from 724 in FY2004 to 64 in FY2010. On 9/11, INTERPOL's Stolen and Lost Travel Document database did not exist.

Visa Security Program

Through VSP, which did not exist on 9/11, ICE, with DOS concurrence, deploys trained special agents overseas to high-risk visa activity posts to identify potential terrorist and criminal threats before they reach the United States. ICE special agents conduct targeted, in-depth reviews of individual visa applications and applicants prior to the issuance of a visa and recommend to consular officers refusal or revocation of applications, when warranted. The VSP is currently deployed to 19 posts in 15 countries.

International Student and Exchange Visitor Program

In addition, ICE manages the International Student and Exchange Visitor Program (SEVP), which tracks and monitors the status and activities of nonimmigrant students and exchange visitors to ensure that only legitimate foreign students or exchange students gain entry to the United States and that they abide by the terms of their visas while here. SEVP also provides timely information about foreign students to several partner agencies, including the Department of State, CBP, and USCIS.

Entry-Exit Screening System

The US-VISIT biometric identity and verification process involves the collection of digital fingerprints and a photograph from international travelers at U.S. visa-issuing posts and ports of entry to help immigration officers determine whether a person is eligible to receive a visa or enter the United States. This information is screened against the DHS IDENT watchlist and is matched with previous biometric data collected from the person, such as during a visa application, to confirm the person is using his/her true identity. To date, DHS has achieved ten-fingerprint collection at entry for 99 percent of air and sea points of entry. Prior to 9/11, inbound travelers' ten-point fingerprints were not collected.

DHS has conducted a number of pilots and studies since 2003 to assess options on how to deploy biometric exit capabilities. These pilots have demonstrated that while the technology exists to collect biometrics, the necessary costs to achieve effective compliance with biometric air exit requirements using currently available technology and processes are high, particularly when compared to any potential security gains.

Accordingly, until a more cost-effective biometric air exit solution becomes available, DHS will continue to implement enhancements to existing biographic air exit systems. These enhancements will focus on strengthening CBP's Advance Passenger Information System information collection and carrier compliance auditing; enhancing US-VISIT's automated matching of arrival and departure records; and posting of "lookouts" for those who have overstayed.

DHS is also undertaking a Department-wide effort to address the backlog of unvetted potential visa overstays, an issue identified by the GAO in its April 2011 report. The goal of this ongoing effort is not only to identify which individuals have overstayed their visas, but also to prioritize identified overstays for removal that may be a threat to national security. Since this effort began, DHS has used automated means to determine that of the 1.6 million potential visa overstays GAO reported in April, 843,000 are no longer in the country. The remaining 757,000 are being vetted in three ways:

- First, US-VISIT, CBP and ICE are screening the overstay leads against CBP's ATS. ATS has the ability to automatically check the records of potential overstays against other databases that can indicate a change in immigration status or a departure from the United States. This information will assist ICE as it prioritizes leads with a potential nexus to national security concerns;

- Second, DHS is providing overstay leads to NCTC to identify additional derogatory information held by the Intelligence Community;

- Third, DHS is leveraging an existing data-sharing arrangement with the Intelligence Community to provide ICE with any additional matches of overstay leads with derogatory information.

This effort has helped to bring about a higher standard of review of overstay leads than previously existed, and at little cost, while enabling ICE to better prioritize targets for investigation and removal. It is a key example of how coordination across the federal government can strengthen frontline operations and national security.

National Security Entry-Exit Registration System

In April 2011, DHS announced the end of the National Security Entry-Exit Registration System (NSEERS) registration process—a critical step forward in the Department's ongoing efforts to eliminate redundancies; streamline the collection of data for individuals entering or exiting the

United States, regardless of nationality; and enhance the capabilities of security personnel working to secure the nation from threats. Since NSEERS was first implemented in 2002, DHS has implemented more robust, risk-based, and intelligence-driven targeting processes. When NSEERS began, DHS received most of its information about an individual when he or she arrived at a port of entry. Today, NSEERS no longer provides a unique security value, as DHS has the ability to obtain information about most individuals before they depart for the United States. Improvements to information collection and analysis capabilities, combined with more robust screening measures for all individuals, have allowed DHS to better address current threats, providing more integrated and effective options for screening individuals for potential ties to terrorism and transnational crime before they enter the United States.

Citizenship and Immigration Documents

USCIS continues to enhance fraud detection and national security capabilities to ensure that immigration benefits are not granted to individuals who pose a threat to national security. USCIS has embedded Fraud Detection and National Security officers in eight other government agencies to increase information sharing and collaboration efforts that enhance law enforcement and intelligence operations. Further, USCIS has implemented a new state-of-the-art system that enhances the verification and sharing of electronic records and has redesigned all of its secure identity documents to comport with the latest DHS and ICAO standards as well as best practices in industry and government.

Since 2009, USCIS has incorporated the use of electronic fingerprints in all of its overseas programs to enhance the accuracy and effectiveness of biometric checks. USCIS is currently working with DOS to pilot a program to use foil technology, which includes a digitized photo of the traveler and other embedded security features, on travel letters issued by USCIS to family members of refugees and asylees to minimize use of fraudulent travel documents to board planes and improve identification of travelers at ports of entry.

The new Permanent Resident Card (commonly referred to as a "green card"), implemented in 2010, includes a radio frequency identification tag that allows CBP to quickly access the electronic records of travelers seeking to enter the United States and includes new security features that reduce the risks of counterfeiting, tampering, and fraud. USCIS has also updated the Employment Authorization Document by adding a machine-readable zone that for the first time allows USCIS to share data with CBP and US-VISIT.

Additionally, USCIS implemented the Secure Mail Initiative to confirm delivery of permanent resident cards and documents pertaining to travel and employment authorization. With USPS tracking information, USCIS customers can stay up-to-date on the delivery status of their documents and USCIS can confirm that these essential documents were delivered to the proper address.

In January 2011, USCIS announced a new tool to enhance the agency's adjudications of certain employment-based immigration petitions known as the Web-based Validation Instrument for Business Enterprises (VIBE). VIBE uses commercially available data to validate basic information about organizations petitioning to employ alien workers. This additional information limits USCIS officers' need to request supplemental evidence directly from petitioning organizations while accelerating the adjudicative vetting process and enhancing the agency's anti-fraud capabilities.

Finally, DHS and DOS have worked with international allies to develop routine sharing of biometric information collected for immigration purposes. These efforts assist in identifying those who travel under multiple identities, or those who conceal their true identity in order to withhold pertinent information in an effort to obtain an immigration benefit. In 2010, DHS began sharing biometric information with the Australia, Canada, New Zealand, and the United Kingdom. To date, this effort has identified many cases of routine immigration fraud, as well as dangerous people traveling under false identities.

Fraudulent Documents

In addition to screening travelers against derogatory information, the U.S. Government has strengthened efforts to detect fraudulent travel documents so that such documents cannot be used by terrorists seeking to subvert the screening process. The ICE Forensic Document Laboratory (FDL) is the federal government's forensic crime laboratory dedicated exclusively to fraudulent document detection and deterrence. USCIS has partnered with the FDL to enhance its capability of identifying fraudulent documents submitted in support of applications and petitions seeking immigration benefits. S&T is currently developing the capability for an officer to capture and send in real time a high resolution image of a suspected fraudulent travel document to the FDL for examination. Additionally, in partnership with DOS, the FDL provides training to international and domestic partners on identifying fraudulent documents.

Drivers License Security

Because many states raised concerns with various aspects of the REAL ID Act of 2005, including implementation costs, privacy issues, and systems capabilities, the Administration strongly supported the "PASS ID Act" legislation in the last Congress to comprehensively address these challenges while maintaining a commitment to driver's license and identification card security. The Administration continues to believe that PASS ID represented the best mechanism for achieving this security goal and fulfilling a key 9/11 Commission recommendation. By replacing the REAL ID requirements of greatest concern to states with more flexible and effective security requirements, PASS ID would enhance driver's license security while safeguarding the privacy of Americans' personal information and reducing the potential burdens on both the states and the public.

Since PASS ID was not enacted, DHS continues to work closely with the States to facilitate REAL ID implementation with a number of states making progress towards meeting REAL ID requirements. The Drivers License Security Grant Program (DLSGP) helps states and territories improve security of state-issued driver's licenses and identification cards in order to reduce fraud, enhance the reliability and accuracy of personal identification documents and prevent terrorism. DHS has awarded over $180 million in DLSGP grants to states and territories since fiscal year 2006 for information technology and facility infrastructure upgrades, document security enhancements, equipment upgrades, and reengineering of business practices. These enhancements have enabled states to make progress toward achieving compliance with many aspects of the REAL ID regulation.

Notwithstanding these efforts, for a number of reasons, including diminished State budgets and uncertainties regarding the prospects of PASS ID legislation in the last Congress, many states have indicated they simply cannot fulfill the REAL ID requirements at this time. To date, 14 states have passed laws mandating noncompliance with REAL ID. Due to these challenges, the Department amended the regulations to give states until January 15, 2013 to comply with REAL ID, the second time the full compliance deadline has been extended. Currently, DHS is preparing guidance for all states clarifying the minimum standards that states must meet to achieve full compliance with REAL ID in order to ensure that every state is afforded the opportunity to reach full compliance in a practical manner.

Transportation Worker Identification Credential Program

Since 2007, DHS has enrolled over 1.9 million port workers and merchant mariners in the TWIC program, a tamper-resistant biometric credential issued to those who require unescorted access to secure areas of ports and vessels.

Biometrics-at-Sea System

The USCG has implemented a mobile biometrics collection system to identify undocumented migrants and match them against known databases of past criminal and immigration violations as well as terrorist watchlists, enabling the USCG to prosecute repeat offenders. Through June 2011, the USCG has identified more than 900 individuals who were enrolled in the US-VISIT database as prior felons, violators of U.S. immigration laws, or other persons of interest and referred to law enforcement authorities for appropriate action.

RECOMMENDATION: Integrate border security into larger network of screening points that includes the transportation system and access to vital facilities[19]

Protecting the nation's borders—land, air, and sea—from the illegal entry of people, weapons, drugs, and contraband is vital to homeland security, as well as economic prosperity. Over the past several years, DHS has deployed unprecedented levels of personnel, technology, and resources to the Southwest border. At the same time, DHS has made critical security improvements along the Northern border, investing in additional Border Patrol agents, technology, and infrastructure while also strengthening efforts to increase the security of the nation's maritime borders.

Southwest Border

Southwest Border Initiative

In March 2009, the Obama Administration launched the Southwest Border Initiative to bring focus and intensity to Southwest border security, coupled with a reinvigorated, smart and effective approach to enforcing immigration laws in the interior of the country.

Over the past two years, the Obama Administration has deployed unprecedented levels of personnel, technology, and resources to the Southwest border. Today, the Border Patrol is better staffed than at any time in its 87-year history. Along the Southwest border, DHS has increased the number of civilian boots on the ground from approximately 9,100 Border Patrol agents in 2001 to more than 17,700 today.

Under the Southwest Border Initiative, DHS has doubled the number of personnel assigned to Border Enforcement Security Task Forces (BESTs), which work to dismantle criminal organizations along the border; increased the number of ICE intelligence analysts along the border focused on cartel violence; quintupled deployments of Border Liaison Officers to work with their Mexican counterparts; begun screening 100 percent of southbound rail shipments for illegal weapons, drugs, and cash; and expanded Unmanned Aircraft System (UAS) coverage to the entire Southwest border. There were no deployments of UASs along the Southwest border prior to 9/11.

Further, the $600 million supplemental requested by the Administration and passed by Congress in 2010 is enabling DHS to continue to add technology, personnel, and infrastructure to the Southwest border. These resources include 1,000 additional Border Patrol Agents; 250 new CBP officers at U.S. ports of entry; 250 new ICE agents focused on transnational crime; improved

---

[19] 9/11 Commission Report, pg. 387

tactical communications systems; two new forward operating bases to improve coordination of border security activities; and additional CBP UASs.

While this work is not done, every key metric currently available shows that these border security efforts are producing significant results. Illegal immigration attempts, as measured by Border Patrol apprehensions, have decreased 36 percent in the past two years, and are less than one third of what they were at their peak. Seizures of drugs, weapons and currency have increased across the board. In fiscal years 2009, 2010, and the first half of 2011, CBP and ICE have seized 75 percent more currency, 31 percent more drugs, and 64 percent more weapons along the Southwest border as compared to two and a half years during the previous administration. Additionally, violent crime in border communities has remained flat or fallen in the past decade—in fact, studies and statistics have shown that some of the safest cities and communities in America are along the Southwest border.

Interagency Efforts

In July 2011, the Obama Administration released its most recent National Southwest Border Counternarcotics Strategy, which provides the Administration's overarching framework to address the threats posed by the illicit narcotics trade. DHS has also forged historic agreements with DOJ, increasing coordination between ICE and the Bureau of Alcohol, Tobacco, Firearms and Explosives and the Drug Enforcement Administration (DEA) on important Southwest border issues such as combating arms trafficking, bolstering information sharing and providing ICE agents the authority to work on important drug trafficking cases.

Further, President Obama authorized the temporary use of up to 1,200 additional National Guard personnel as a bridge to longer-term enhancements in border protection and law enforcement personnel from DHS to target illicit networks' trafficking in people, drugs, illegal weapons, money, and the violence associated with these illegal activities. That support has allowed DHS to bridge the gap and hire the additional agents funded in the FY 2010 Border security supplemental to support efforts along the Southwest Border.

In partnership with the DEA and DOD, the Administration stood up the new Border Intelligence Fusion Section within the El Paso Intelligence Center, which provides a comprehensive Southwest Border Common Intelligence picture, as well as real-time operational intelligence, to law enforcement partners in the region—further streamlining and enhancing operations.

Research and Development

DHS' S&T Directorate is currently developing and testing new technologies along the Southern and Northern borders, including:

- *Personnel Detection Sensors* – To detect human activity in storm drains and sewers, which are being used as conduits for illegal activity;

- *Renewable Energy for Video Surveillance* – To increase intrusion detection in the remote areas of the border that have no available power;

- *Automated Camera System* – To alert operators of anomalies in order to increase detections of suspicious activity;

- *Buried Border Cable Tripwire* – To detect illegal crossings between points of entry;

- *Airborne Wide Area Surveillance Technology* – To improve the detection and tracking of low-flier aircraft; and

- *Mobile Surveillance System Upgrades* – To enhance radar and image capabilities used to detect border crossings.

Collaboration with State and Local Law Enforcement

The federal government has worked closely with state and local law enforcement along the border, serving together on task forces, conducting joint operations, providing the latest intelligence, and coordinating operational priorities.

DHS has increased the funding state and local law enforcement can use to combat border-related crime through Operation Stonegarden—a DHS grant program designed to support state and local law enforcement efforts along the border. Based on risk, cross-border traffic, and border-related threat intelligence, 82 percent of 2009 and 2010 Operation Stonegarden funding went to Southwest border states.

Because partnerships with federal, state and local law enforcement agencies, as well as the private sector, remain critical to the Department's overall success, DHS has initiated new programs to increase collaboration; enhance intelligence and information sharing; and develop coordinated operational plans. One example is the Alliance to Combat Transnational Threats, which utilizes a collaborative enforcement approach to leverage the capabilities and resources of DHS in partnership with more than 60 law enforcement agencies in Arizona and the Government of Mexico to deter, disrupt, and interdict individuals and criminal organizations that pose a threat to the United States.

Additionally, the Joint Harbor Operations Center at USCG Sector San Diego, established in 2004, is a multi-agency command center that coordinates maritime law enforcement operations, including the interdiction of the illegal movement of people and drugs across the maritime border. This unified command includes representatives from the USCG, CBP, ICE, the U.S. Navy, Joint Task Force-North, the California National Guard and local law enforcement.

ICE also continues to expand its BESTs, which were first established in 2005 to bring together federal, state, local, and foreign law enforcement to identify, disrupt and dismantle criminal organizations which pose significant threats to border security. There are currently 21 BESTs throughout the United States, including 11 along the Southwest border.

Increased Cooperation with Mexico

Reflecting unprecedented collaboration, Secretary Napolitano and her Mexican counterparts have signed numerous bilateral agreements and declarations to bolster and deepen collaboration in the areas of enforcement, planning, information and intelligence sharing, joint operations, and trade facilitation along the Southwest border. DHS is also working with Mexican and other federal partners to implement Presidents Obama and Calderon's Declaration on 21st Century Border Management, pursuing initiatives and programs designed to expedite the legitimate flow of people and goods and focus law enforcement resources on those people and goods that represent the highest risk or about which officials know the least.

DHS- through CBP, ICE and USCG- coordinates joint operations and information sharing along the Southwest border with Mexico. For example, ICE and the Government of Mexico have entered into a Criminal History Information Sharing Arrangement in which ICE provides serious felony conviction information on Mexican nationals being repatriated to Mexico. Further, through the Illegal Drug Program, ICE refers narcotics smuggling cases declined for prosecution in the United States to the Mexican Office of the Attorney General for prosecution.

In order to help disrupt the movement of criminal proceeds from the United States to Mexico, the Office of Counternarcotics Enforcement, ICE, and the Government of Mexico for the first time collaborated in April 2009 on the Bi-National Criminal Proceeds Study, which describes the criminal proceeds supply chain and quantifies important indicators of this illegal financial network. As a result of the enhanced intelligence on the movement of illicit funds, ICE assisted in the seizure of over $170 million from the Pacific Rim Cartel, a ring of drug traffickers that operate from locations along the Pacific coast. Further, ICE and the Government of Mexico have initiated over 50 joint financial investigations, made over 100 arrests in both United States and Mexico, and seized over $23.5 million in illicit proceeds within the United States.

To increase information sharing, the United States and Mexico are establishing a new cross-border communications network, which will improve incident response and coordination among participating federal, state, and local law enforcement and public safety personnel along the border. In addition, the Department is increasing joint training programs with Mexican law enforcement agencies—focusing on money laundering, human trafficking, fraudulent documents and visa recognition, and customs enforcement.

Northern Border

The U.S.-Canada border presents unique security challenges based on geography, weather, and the immense volume of trade and travel. At over 5,500 miles, the border spans diverse terrains and climates, metropolitan areas and vast open spaces. Roughly 300,000 people and $1.5 billion in trade cross the northern border every day, representing the largest bilateral flows of goods and people in the world.

The Obama Administration has made significant advancements in creating a secure and resilient Northern border. DHS continues to invest in personnel, technology, and infrastructure, and to strengthen cooperation with federal, state/provincial, tribal, and private sector partners on both sides of the border. These achievements have resulted in a more secure Northern border that facilitates legitimate travel and trade.

Personnel, Technology and Infrastructure

DHS has made important security improvements along the Northern border, investing in additional Border Patrol agents, technology, and infrastructure. Currently, CBP has more than 2,200 Border Patrol agents on the Northern border, a 500 percent increase since 9/11. CBP also has nearly 3,700 CBP Officers managing the flow of people and goods across ports of entry and crossings along the Northern border. In addition, CBP is using Recovery Act funds to modernize more than 35 land ports of entry along the Northern border to meet current security and operational needs.

The Department has also continued to deploy technology along the Northern border, including thermal camera systems, Mobile Surveillance Systems, and Remote Video Surveillance Systems, and successfully completed the first long-range CBP Predator-B unmanned aircraft patrol under expanded Federal Aviation Administration authorization that extends the range of approved airspace along the Northern border. Approximately 950 miles along the Northern border from Washington to Minnesota are currently covered by unmanned aircraft, in addition to approximately 200 miles along the northern border in New York and Lake Ontario—none of which were covered prior to the creation of DHS.

Strong Partnerships with Canada

In February 2011, President Obama and Prime Minister Harper announced a landmark "Shared Vision for Perimeter Security and Economic Competitiveness" that sets forth how the two countries will manage shared homeland and economic security in the 21st century. This "Shared Vision" emphasizes shared responsibility for the safety, security, and resilience of the United States and Canada. This approach focuses on addressing threats at the earliest point possible; facilitating trade, economic growth, and jobs; collaborating on integrated cross-border law enforcement; and partnering to secure and strengthen the resilience of critical infrastructure and cybersecurity.

Through the Integrated Cross-Border Maritime Law Enforcement Operations Shiprider agreement, DHS and Canada can leverage joint law enforcement efforts to bolster cross-border security operations. This agreement enables the Royal Canadian Mounted Police, USCG, CBP, and ICE to cross-train, share resources and personnel, and utilize each others' vessels in the waters of both countries. The Border Patrol, ICE, USCG, Canadian law enforcement, and other federal partners also collaborate through Integrated Border Enforcement Teams, which work to identify, investigate, and interdict individuals and organizations that may pose a threat to national security or are engaged in organized criminal activity along the Northern border.

In 2010, ICE, CBP and CBSA signed a memorandum of understanding to promote the sharing of currency seizure information between law enforcement agencies in order to improve their ability to identify potential threats and assist in money-laundering and terrorist-financing investigations.

In addition, in 2010, DHS and Public Safety Canada announced a first of its kind plan to establish a comprehensive cross-border approach to critical infrastructure resilience. As part of this plan, DHS and Transport Canada conducted vulnerability assessments on shared bridges between the United States and Canada, providing recommended mitigation strategies to prioritize resources and guard against known threats.

Maritime Border Security

As the lead agency for maritime border security, the USCG works with other federal, state, local and tribal partners to enhance security along the U.S. maritime border and uses interagency partnerships and international bilateral agreements to accomplish this mission.

The USCG's overarching strategy is to increase maritime border security through a layered security system that begins beyond the country's physical borders. At-sea presence deters potential threats, provides mobile surveillance coverage, increases warning time, engages smugglers at the earliest point possible, and enables USCG to address potential threats before they can cause harm to the United States.

USCG's Maritime Security and Response Operations include waterborne and aerial patrols as well as armed escorts of hazardous cargos and passenger vessels in order to reduce the risk of terrorism to the U.S. Marine Transportation System and CIKR. The USCG also utilizes advanced capabilities to interdict identified threats—including chemical, biological, radiological, nuclear, and explosives threats—before they reach the United States.

USCG has increased the presence and capabilities of maritime forces to address high risk threats through the establishment of the Deployable Operations Group, which can respond rapidly to terrorist and weapons of mass destruction threats as well as Maritime Safety and Security Teams at critical U.S. ports, which focus on domestic maritime threats and post-incident response.

DHS's S&T Directorate is also pursuing new technologies to enhance detection of small maritime vessels and submersibles, in accordance with the National Small Vessels Security Strategy. S&T recently delivered new technologies to the Joint Inter Agency Task Force – South to help better predict when and where to look for submersibles traveling from South America into U.S. waters. Further, DHS is working with the National Oceanic and Atmospheric Administration (NOAA) to leverage currently deployed NOAA coastal radars for the purpose of detecting and tracking small maritime vessels.

Ensuring Robust Privacy and Civil Rights and Civil Liberties Safeguards

RECOMMENDATIONS: Safeguard Individual Privacy When Sharing Information[20] and Maintain Civil Liberties While Protecting Security[21]

The Department involves its Privacy Office and Office for Civil Rights and Civil Liberties (CRCL) from the outset of the policymaking process, building in privacy and civil rights and civil liberties protections into all of its operations, policies and technology deployments.

DHS's Privacy Office is the first statutorily required privacy office of any federal agency. The office partners with privacy staff in every component of the Department to assess all new or proposed programs, systems, technologies, or rule-makings for privacy risks, and recommends privacy protections when personally identifiable information is collected, used, shared, or maintained by the Department. The Privacy Office also publishes compliance documentation like System of Record Notices and Privacy Impact Assessments and participates in U.S. Government-wide policy initiatives governing information sharing programs like fusion centers.

CRCL supports the Department's mission to secure the nation while preserving individual liberty, fairness, and equality under the law. CRCL created a Civil Rights and Civil Liberties Impact Assessment process to review Departmental programs, and conducts regular community engagement with stakeholder communities, elected officials, and non-governmental organizations across the country.

CRCL and the Privacy Office provide training on privacy, civil rights and civil liberties to DHS intelligence professionals assigned to fusion centers and to state and local fusion center personnel. The DHS Privacy Office also reviews fusion center privacy policies to ensure that they adhere to the standards established in the Information Sharing Environment Privacy Guidelines. All officially-designated fusion centers currently have approved privacy policies.

The Department has also incorporated strong privacy and civil rights and civil liberties standards into its cybersecurity programs and initiatives. Personnel receive specific training on the protection of privacy and civil liberties as they relate to computer network security activities. Additionally, as part of the landmark agreement signed by Secretary Napolitano and Secretary of Defense Robert Gates in October 2010 to align and enhance America's capabilities to protect against threats to critical civilian and military computer systems and networks, DHS has sent privacy, civil liberties and legal personnel to DOD's National Security Agency to ensure the protection of fundamental rights.

---

[20] 9/11 Commission Report, pg. 394
[21] 9/11 Commission Report, pg. 394-395

Conclusion

Ten years after the September 11, 2001 attacks, the work of the Department of Homeland Security is ongoing and many challenges remain. Nonetheless, our country is stronger than it was on 9/11.

Over the past ten years, we have made great strides to secure our nation against a large attack or disaster, to protect critical infrastructure and cyber networks, and to engage a broader range of Americans in the shared responsibility for security. We are also a more prepared and resilient nation, able to bounce back and rebuild stronger after a major crisis or disaster.

There are many people to thank for the milestones outlined in this report, including former Homeland Security Secretaries Tom Ridge and Michael Chertoff; the 9/11 Commission, particularly Chair and Vice Chair Thomas Kean and Lee Hamilton; the Congressional Homeland Security Committees, particularly Senators Joseph Lieberman and Susan Collins and Representatives Peter King and Bennie Thompson; as well as many others.

Most of all, credit goes to the men and women of DHS and the law enforcement officers and emergency management professionals who work on the frontlines everyday protecting our country, at home and abroad. Their dedication is constant and unparalleled.

Acronym Listing

Below is the list of acronyms used in the report.

ACAMS: Automated Critical Asset Management System
AIT – Advanced Imaging Technology
API – Advanced Passenger Information
ATS –Advanced Targeting System
AWW – America's Waterway Watch Program
BEST – Border Enforcement Security Task Force
CAPTAP – Critical Infrastructure Asset Protection Technical Assistance Program
CAT/ BPSS – Credential Authentication Technology / Boarding Pass Scanning System
CBSA – Canada Border Services Agency
CBP – U.S. Customs and Border Protection
CFATS – Chemical Facility Anti-Terrorism Standards
CIKR – Critical Infrastructure and Key Resources
CIKR ISE – Critical Infrastructure and Key Resources Information Sharing Environment
CSI – Container Security Initiative
CRCL – Office for Civil Rights and Civil Liberties
C-TPAT – Customs Trade Partnership Against Terrorism
CVE – Countering Violent Extremism
DEA – U.S. Drug Enforcement Administration
DHS – U.S. Department of Homeland Security
DHS TRIP – DHS Travel Redress Inquiry Program
DLSGP – Drivers License Security Grant Program
DNDO – Domestic Nuclear Detection Office
DOD – U.S. Department of Defense
DOE – U.S. Department of Energy
DOJ – U.S. Department of Justice
DOS – U.S. Department of State
DOT – U.S. Department of Transportation
ECTF – Electronic Crimes Task Force Program
EDL – Enhanced Driver's License
EDS – Explosive Detection System
ESTA – Electronic System for Travel Authorization
ETC – Enhanced Tribal Cards
ETD – Explosives Trace Detection
FBI – Federal Bureau of Investigation
FDNS – Fraud Detection and National Security Directorate
FDL – Forensic Document Laboratory
FEMA – Federal Emergency Management Agency
GLANSER – Geospatial Location Accountability and Navigation Systems for Emergency Responders
GAO- Government Accountability Office

GNDA – Global Nuclear Detection Architecture
I&A – DHS Office of Intelligence and Analysis
IATA – International Air Transport Association
ICAO – International Civil Aviation Organization
ICE – U.S. Immigration and Customs Enforcement
ICS – Incident Command System
IED – Improvised Explosive Device
IICS - Infrastructure Information Collection System
IMAT – Incident Management Assistance Team
IMO – International Maritime Organization
IP – DHS Office of Infrastructure Protection
IPS – International Port Security Program
JTTF – Joint Terrorism Task Force
MSRAM – Maritime Security Risk Analysis Model
NCCIC – National Cybersecurity and Communications Integration Center
NCPS – National Cybersecurity Protection System
NCSD – National Cyber Security Division
NCTC – National Counterterrorism Center
NECP – National Emergency Communications Plan
NNFED – National Nuclear Forensics Expertise Development
NIPP – National Infrastructure Protection Plan
NLE – National Level Exercise
NOAA – National Oceanic and Atmospheric Administration
NPPD – National Protection and Programs Directorate
NSEERS – National Security Entry-Exit Registration System
NSI – Nationwide Suspicious Activity Reporting Initiative
NTAS – National Terrorism Advisory System
NTNFC – National Technical Nuclear Forensics Center
OEC – DHS Office of Emergency Communications
PCIIMS: Protected Critical Infrastructure Information Management System
PCSC – Preventing and Combating Serious Crime
PNR – Passenger Name Records
PS-Prep™ – Voluntary Private Sector Preparedness Accreditation and Certification Program
PSA – Protective Security Advisor
S&T – DHS Science and Technology Directorate
SAR – Suspicious Activities Reporting
SECURE – System Efficacy through Commercialization, Utilization, Relevance and Evaluation
SEVP – Student and Exchange Visitor Program
SHSGP – State Homeland Security Grant Program
STC – Securing the Cities
STSPA – Surface Transportation Security Priority Assessment
TIC – Trusted Internet Connection
TSA – Transportation Security Administration
TSC – Terrorist Screening Center
TSDB – Terrorist Screening Database
TSO- Transportation Security Officer

TWIC – Transportation Worker Identification Credential
UAS – Unmanned Aircraft System
UASI – Urban Areas Security Initiative
US-CERT – U.S. Computer Emergency Readiness Team
USCG – U.S. Coast Guard
USCIS – U.S. Citizenship and Immigration Services
USPS – U.S. Postal Service
USSS – U.S. Secret Service
US-VISIT – U.S. Visitor and Immigrant Status Indicator Technology Program
VIBE – Validation Instrument for Business Enterprises
VIPR – Visible Intermodal Prevention and Response Teams
VSP – Visa Security Program
VWP – Visa Waiver Program
WCO – World Customs Organization
WHTI – Western Hemisphere Travel Initiative